IN HARM'S WAY

IN HARM'S WAY

THE DYNAMICS OF URBAN VIOLENCE

JAVIER AUYERO
AND
MARÍA FERNANDA BERTI

PRINCETON UNIVERSITY PRESS
PRINCETON AND OXFORD

Published by Princeton University Press, 41 William Street,
Princeton, New Jersey 08540
In the United Kingdom: Princeton University Press, 6 Oxford Street,
Woodstock, Oxfordshire OX20 1TW
press.princeton.edu
Excerpt from *Let the Great World Spin* © 2009 by Colum McCann. Pub-
lished by HarperCollins Publishers Ltd. © Colum McCann, 2009, *Let the
Great World Spin* and Bloomsbury Publishing Plc. © Colum McCann, 2009,
Let the Great World Spin Penguin and Random House. All Rights Reserved.

Library of Congress Cataloging-in-Publication Data

Auyero, Javier.
   In harm's way : the dynamics of urban violence / Javier Auyero and Maria
Fernanda Berti.
      pages cm
   Includes bibliographical references and index.
   ISBN 978-0-691-16477-9 (hardback)
   1. Urban violence—Argentina—Buenos Aires.   2. Urban poor—Ar-
gentina—Buenos Aires.   3. Marginality, Social—Argentina—Buenos
Aires.   4. Buenos Aires (Argentina)—Social conditions.   I. Berti, María
Fernanda, 1972–   II. Title.

HN270.B8A98 2015
   303.609173'2098212—dc23
2014049576

British Library Cataloging-in-Publication Data is available
This book has been composed in Adobe Caslon Pro and Avenir LT Std
Printed on acid-free paper. ∞
Printed in the United States of America
10 9 8 7 6 5 4 3 2 1

**TO
OUR
STUDENTS**

But it was ridiculous, really. How could her mother have crawled away from that life and started anew? How could she have walked away intact? With what, sweeping brooms, dust pans? Here we go, honey, grab my high-heeled boots, put them in the wagon, westward we go. Stupid, she knew.

Colum McCann,
Let the Great World Spin

CONTENTS

ILLUSTRATIONS

PREFACE

In Argentina, and elsewhere in Latin America, members of the middle and upper-middle classes tend to be the main spokespeople in public debates regarding the issue of citizens' public safety (*seguridad*). Public discourse about urban violence tends to be dominated by those occupying privileged positions in the social structure; they are the ones who talk most about the issue because, presumably, they are the ones most affected by it. And yet any cursory count of the victims of urban violence in the subregion tells us that those who are suffering the most from it live (and die) at the bottom of the sociosymbolic order. But the inhabitants of the urban margins are hardly ever heard from in debates about public safety. They live *en la inseguridad*, but the discourse about violence and risk belongs to—in other words, it is manufactured and manipulated by—others. As a result, the experience of interpersonal violence among the urban poor becomes something unspeakable, and the everyday fear and trauma lived in relegated territories is constantly muted and denied. The urban violence among those who suffer from it the most is banished from public debate.

In a very basic sense, this book is about the collective trauma created by the constant and implacable interpersonal violence in a marginalized neighborhood in the outskirts of the city of Buenos Aires, Argentina. We want to subject the experience of violence to social scientific analysis and, given the incessant disavowal of its very existence, we also want to unearth those lived experiences so that they can become both visible and a subject of debate. Our modest attempt to go against the persistent silencing and denial is why we devote a large portion of this book to the basic documentation of the multiple forms of violence that exist at the urban margins.

In the course of our research and writing, we struggled with the proper way of representing interpersonal brutality among the dispossessed. The stories we reconstruct and the testimonies we cite could be used to reproduce and reinforce the most pernicious stereotypes about the urban poor. A superficial—or ill-intended—reading of the ethnographic material presented here could lead readers to think that residents of the place where we conducted our fieldwork are, to cite the film title of Ettore Scola's savage comedy, *Brutti, Sporchi e Cattivi* (*Ugly, Dirty and Bad*). More or less euphemistic versions of this accusatory stigma abound in the social sciences, and every now and then reemerge, as we can see with the renewed interest in the now sanitized notion of the "culture of poverty." The reason why this stigma persists despite rigorous sociological and anthropological research that debunks it is beyond the scope of this book. But we are very aware that a selective appropriation of the material presented below—the image of a house perched over a putrid stream, the reconstruction of a violent assault or a domestic fight—could be enough to trigger a damning stigmatization of those living on the lower rungs of the social ladder. Even despite best intentions, academics and journalists can join the symbolic war against the folks they most care about, in our case, those constantly living at risk at the urban margins in contemporary Argentina. For that reason, while writing this book, we oftentimes hesitated. We wrote entire sections, and then, fearful of the way in which we imagined they would be read, got rid of them. And yet, the person who is in daily direct contact with the children and adolescents of the area (Fernanda) cannot afford the luxury—the academic privilege, one could say—of indecision. "This needs to be told now," Fernanda wrote in her diary at the end of a particularly taxing day in front of the classroom. It was this sense of urgency, and not an intellectual epiphany, that made us suspend our doubts and representational worries, and pushed us to write the pages that follow.

IN HARM'S WAY

INTRODUCTION

The afternoon begins; I take attendance. Maitén comes close to me and says, at a whisper, that she is not coming tomorrow.[1] "They shot at my brother in Villa Ceferina yesterday. He is in the hospital; he's doing pretty good. Tomorrow I'm not coming." I don't write this conversation down in my field note journal. I don't bring my notebook anymore. But I listen. I continue taking attendance. Next to my desk Osvaldo and Sami are seated. "Show it to teacher, come on, show her! She's not gonna say anything," says Sami to Osvaldo. I ask Sami what's going on, and he pulls a bullet out of his pocket. "I found it on the sidewalk in front of my house, when I was coming here." Ricardo chimes in, "it must be from last night . . . you could feel shots all around." I ask them, without knowing, if it's used. "No teacher, see? It has to be missing this part! It's not used . . . it's one from a .9 mm."

I had my camera in my bag. I brought it because I am photographing my sixth grade students to make them a graduation video. I took out my camera and photographed the bullet. Sami asks, "Are you going to show the photos to my mom? Are you going to put them on the Internet?" "Why are you taking photos?" they asked. I responded, "Do you remember Javier, the man who came a couple of months ago to our class? Well . . . he and I are finishing a book together about the life of the neighborhood. Remember when I told you about that? We would like to tell the story of this bullet."

Fernanda's Field Notes, November 27, 2012

August 2012. It was not in our plans to visit Lucho's grave, but the insistence with which his closest friends and family spoke about the objects and mementos left there persuaded us. One gray Saturday, with an overcast sky and a persistent drizzle, we took the 219 bus from a city center in the southern part of the Conurbano Bonaerense and made the trip to the cemetery on Belgrano Street.[2] In the information office, close to the main entrance, a retired policeman showed us where we should ask about the grave's location. Out of curiosity, and maybe out of boredom, he asked us for whom we were looking. We told him Luis Alberto Orijuela, a young man who had been one of our students at the Arquitecto Tucci elementary school. With a fixed look, in the almost empty waiting room, he said something to us that, in more than one way, succinctly expresses the concern that fills the pages of this book: "More and more the young ones are dying."

"Section 23, Row 1, Grave 71," the clerk informed us. The policeman showed us the path. We couldn't remember the last time we had been in the cemetery, and we took note of the loud colors of many of the more recent graves (blue and yellow for those who in life had been Boca Juniors fans; red and white for those of River Plate; there were also graves with the colors of San Lorenzo, Independiente, and other soccer clubs). It was not easy for us to find Lucho. His grave is in the section farthest from the entrance, where signs are scarce. After more than half an hour trying to find it, we asked for help from a worker who was passing by on a bicycle. "Here it is. Now next time, you'll know where to find it," he said to us kindly before continuing on his way.

Lucho was seventeen when he was assassinated. On his tomb, painted with the red and white of River Plate, colorful flowers lived alongside empty bottles of alcohol and messages from his friends and family: "You have given me so much affection, and we have shared so many good memories, that it is

FIGURE 1. Lucho's grave.

truly beautiful to remember you," "We miss you, we miss you so much, you were the rock that supported us, through the good and the bad, in times of happiness and sadness." Far from there, in Arquitecto Tucci, on the wall facing the house where Lucho lived all his short life, his friends painted: "Lucho, we will never forget you" (figure 1).

We stayed a long while before his grave, in silence. A funeral proceeded nearby. Judging by the age of those who were there, they, too, cried for a young death. One of us, Fernanda, had met Lucho some years ago, when he was her student at School 98 in Tucci. She remembered him as a boy with a charming smile and a precious face, one with handsome dark features that seduced more than one girl in the school. He didn't like to attend class, and he did little in the classroom, but he wasn't a mischievous boy, at least not when he was with Fernanda. Always with his cap on—the same hat his family members would place in a small glass case in his tomb—he usually sat at the back of the classroom and paid little attention to the day's lesson. Fernanda had him as a student the year after his mother passed. Reina had suffered from a long and tortuous bout of uterine cancer. Members of the staff at the school still remember the collections they raised to help her with the cost of the cabs that took her to Pena hospital, and the repeated "nos" of some drivers because of the sudden hemorrhages that Reina often had in route. Lucho many times said to his teacher, "I miss my mom."

Fernanda stopped seeing Lucho after he finished sixth grade. However, she kept in touch by way of two of his six siblings, Alvaro and Samuel, who were also students of hers, and through other students that knew him. The rumors about Lucho's criminal activities were documented in the field journal in which Fernanda, over the course of thirty months, registered the stories of her students: "Lucho is stealing," "He's stealing at the Salada market with another guy from the neighborhood," "He has three motorcycles, all stolen."

The night of February 29, 2012, Lucho received multiple shots to his thorax and extremities. He died shortly after arriving at Redael Hospital. The stories about his death are varied, and we could never corroborate them. We do know that at the moment in which we write this, there is one suspect detained for trial, a thirty-year-old man and a neighbor of Tucci. According to his family and some of his friends, Lucho was killed by a gang from outside the neighborhood that was looking for someone else. Even though she recognizes Lucho's short criminal career, the new partner of his father, Luna, tells us, "He was starting to save himself [*rescatarse*] . . . he had a girlfriend, and they were awaiting a baby . . . That's why he wanted to save himself." In the family's version, Lucho was in the wrong place at the wrong time. According to others, some of them students of Fernanda, "Lucho was stealing at the fair, he jacked bags of clothes, he robbed the buses [that brought in merchandise]. With that he bought drugs . . . he got killed by some guys that wouldn't let him steal there anymore."

The wake was in his home. In an open casket, he wore not the jersey of his favorite soccer club, River Plate, but that of Estudiantes de la Plata. "It's that he liked that one, he liked that one because it was original, the only official club jersey he had," his friends told us, and then they insisted that we go visit him in the cemetery. A few days after that visit, Luna sent us photos of Lucho's newborn baby boy from her cell phone. In the text message, she wrote, "See how cute?!"

Fifteen months after Lucho's death, on November 14, 2012, Lucho's brother Samuel told Fernanda that "yesterday two drug dealers killed two friends of Lucho's," apparently after they had stolen a motorcycle. After the story of the death of his brother's friends, Samuel added, "in my neighborhood not one, not one is left . . . they are killing them all."

September 2011. In the classroom where Fernanda teaches, Chaco colors a new version of his favorite drawing: *el pibe chorro*, the thief kid (figure 2). The drawing mixes the style of Japanese comics with the aesthetic of the Conurbano Bonaerense: the boy, with a challenging look, striped T-shirt, and ripped pants, holds a revolver in his right hand.

FIGURE 2. *Pibe chorro.*

"This is a .22," Chaco shows Fernanda. At thirteen he already knows how to distinguish between a .9, a .22, a .38, and a .45. "They are very different. My uncle has a 22. I sometimes go with him when he goes out to rob. I go as the lookout. Did I tell you that my other uncle was killed by the police? He was robbing a bus."

At the end of the year, Chaco will receive his primary school diploma, even though he is only at the level of a fourth grader. He spends his days at school listening to music (*cumbia* and *regatón*) on his cell phone.

Chaco, his four siblings, and their mother live in a house of exposed brick with a roof of corrugated iron sheets. There he shares a small room with his siblings. Tatiana, his mother, works as a domestic worker in the city of Buenos Aires. From Monday to Saturday, she leaves very early, before Chaco gets up to go to school; she returns around nine at night, a short time before Chaco goes to sleep. With the salary of a domestic worker, supplemented by a government social program, they just barely make it to the end of the month.

Chaco's world is one of emotional and material shortages, and also a universe in which interpersonal violence makes itself present with intermittent, but brutal, frequency. Not only in his neighborhood, Arquitecto Tucci, where, according to him, "they're all drug dealers, they shoot each other up every day," but also in his home. "I want to see him dead," Chaco says about his father. "In the house we don't have anything, and he does nothing. He sleeps all day. He drinks a lot. And he fights with my mom." Tatiana suffered the rage of her drunkard partner more than once. "Last time he almost killed her," Chaco shares. A neighbor of Chaco's family described the domestic quarrel: "The guy dragged her by the hair through the street, and he cursed her out at the top of his lungs. Thankfully, a neighbor saved her. She had bad luck. She cooks for him, she washes the clothes, and he's a good-for-nothing. He says he's a taxi driver, but he doesn't do anything." Chaco remembers perfectly the last time he saw his father: "Since she ran after him with a blade, he hasn't shown up. It's better that he doesn't ever come back."

The turbulent world in which Chaco lives and is growing up may explain his countless threats to his classmates: "I'm gonna blow you away," "I'm gonna shoot you in the head," he yells at them, pretending to have a gun in his hands. And maybe it also helps to explain the destiny he believes he has, a future similar to that of the thieving kids he sketches so well. "Miss," he says to his teacher, "one day you're gonna see me on TV. I'm gonna rob a bank and they're gonna fill me with bullets. You're gonna see me; I'm gonna be killed by the police."

Lucho's tragic death and Chaco's life illustrate some of the different forms of violence that encircle the lives of the urban poor in contemporary Buenos Aires. The *hows* and *whys* of the copresence and concatenations of these *violences* among the marginalized are the subjects of this book.

VIOLENCE IN URBAN LATIN AMERICA

In the last two decades, most countries in Latin America have witnessed a sharp increase in new forms of interpersonal violence (Koonings 2001; Koonings and Kruijt 2007; Rodgers et al. 2012; Programa de las Naciones Unidas para el Desarrollo [PNUD] 2013). Although violence has had a continual presence in the history of the subcontinent (Imbusch, Misse, and Carrión 2011), the recent skyrocketing of brutality is considered a key threat, besieging many of the newly established democracies in the region (Arias and Goldstein 2010; Pearce 2010; Jones and Rodgers 2009; Caldeira 2000).

Although the "newness" of this violence has been the subject of much scholarly debate among academics (see, for example, Hume 2009; Wilding 2010), most agree that the region has seen a significant change since the early 1990s in the prevalent forms of violence. This recent violence is "increasingly available to a variety of social actors," is no longer an exclusive "resource of elites or security forces," and includes "everyday criminal and street violence, riots, social cleansing, private account selling, police arbitrariness, paramilitary activities, post–Cold War guerrillas, etc." (Koonings 2001:403). As Peter Imbusch, Michel Misse, and Fernando Carrión assert in their comprehensive review of violence research in the region, political violence "has now receded significantly in most countries of the continent" (2011:95), while other forms have multiplied (i.e., interpersonal violence, drug-related violence, domestic abuse, child abuse, and sexual assault). These forms of violence are quite varied and, in contrast with past modes, are now located mostly in urban areas.

Contrary to public discourse that frames "public insecurity" as a sort of disease affecting everybody in equal ways, this "new" urban violence is highly stratified. It impacts the most disadvantaged populations in disproportionate ways (Gay 2005; Brinks 2008; Centro de Estudios Legales y Sociales [CELS] 2009), particularly adolescents and young adults (Imbusch, Misse, and Carrión 2011), both as victims and as perpetrators. Most of this violence, furthermore, is concentrated within the poor neighborhoods, slums, and shantytowns of the region (Moser and McIlawine 2004; for Rio de Janeiro, see Gay 2005, Perlman 2010, Wilding 2010, and Penglase 2010; for Santiago, see Lunecke 2008; for Managua, see Rodgers 2006, 2009; for Medellín, see Ponce de León-Calero 2014; for Guatemala, see O'Neill and Thomas 2011) to the point of becoming "the defining feature of life in such settlements at the beginning of the 21st century" (Rodgers et al. 2012:15). It is in one of these "territories of urban relegation" (Wacquant 2008) that one of us works as an elementary schoolteacher and where—sometimes together, other times individually, other times with the help of research assistants—we conducted thirty months of ethnographic fieldwork focusing on the uses and forms of interpersonal violence.

Buenos Aires is no exception to this stratified depacification of daily life. There, the increase of social and criminal violence is beyond dispute (Observatorio de la Deuda Social Argentina [ODSA] 2011). Official data for the province of

Buenos Aires, for example, show a doubling of crime rates between 1995 and 2008, from 1,114 to 2,010 criminal episodes
per 100,000 residents and from 206 to 535 crimes against persons per 100,000 residents (Dirección Nacional de Política Criminal [DNPC] 2008). Sexual and domestic abuse has also been
on the rise during the last two decades.[3]

Different from general treatments of increasing crime and
violence in the region and/or some particular cities (see PNUD
2013), this book focuses on a specific social universe, a concrete
locality, where interpersonal violence is marked by "an exces-
siveness which allows us better to perceive the facts than in
those places where, although no less essential, they still remain
small-scale and involuted" (Mauss 1979 [1916]). The poor neighborhood we call Arquitecto Tucci has been a "hot spot" of criminal activity for more than a decade. Fifteen years ago, a journalistic report on the neighborhood cited police sources that
mentioned the high occurrence of crime in the area (Torresi
1998). However, these days violent crime has reached unprecedented levels. According to the municipal Defensoría General, homicides in Arquitecto Tucci increased 180 percent since
2007—from a total number of seventeen in that year to forty-
eight between January and October 2012 alone (the population of the municipality where Arquitecto Tucci is located
grew only 4.2 percent between 2001 and 2010). The murder
rate in Arquitecto Tucci is thus 28.4 per 100,000 residents—
four times that of the state of Buenos Aires. The population of
Arquitecto Tucci is roughly 28 percent of the total population
of the municipal district (pop. 600,000). Yet out of a total sixty-
five homicides that took place in the municipal district during
2012, 58 percent occurred in Arquitecto Tucci (Corte Suprema
de Justicia de la Nación [CSJN] 2013).[4]

Physicians who have been working in the emergency rooms
at the local hospital and local health center confirm the skyrocketing of interpersonal violence in Tucci. "Today," says a doc-

tor with fifteen years of experience in the district, "it is much more common to attend to patients with injuries provoked by gunshots or knives . . . at least one per day." The director of the emergency room at the local hospital that serves the population of Arquitecto Tucci seconds this general impression: during the last decade, he says, there has been a 10 percent annual increase in the number of those wounded by gunshots or knives (*heridos por armas de fuego y arma blanca*). The figures provided by the emergency room at the main public hospital in the neighborhood confirmed this assessment. During 2010, physicians there attended to 109 injured by knives and 191 injured by gunshots (90 percent of them were men younger than twenty-five). This represents a 10 percent increase from 2009.

Although no official figures exist, interviews with social workers and teachers at the local school indicate that sexual violence and physical aggression between family members and intimate partners have also intensified. If we are to avoid reproducing the "masculinist silences" (Hume 2009) implicit in the ways in which violence is measured, attention to homicide and public violence data should be complemented with an equal consideration of these other forms of interpersonal violence, such as sexual and/or domestic aggression. In the pages that follow, we examine the ways in which public and private violence(s) (drug-related violence, street violence, intimate violence) overlap, intersect, and, in doing so, blur these very boundaries.

VIOLENCE AT THE URBAN MARGINS: AN ETHNOGRAPHIC RECONSTRUCTION

This book examines the sources, uses, and forms of interpersonal violence in the everyday life of men and women, adults and children, living in a marginalized neighborhood in contemporary Argentina. It also scrutinizes the manifold ways in which the routines and practices they devise serve to cope and deal with this overwhelming violence. For the purposes of the analysis that follows, we adopt a modified version of the World Health Organization's (WHO) definition of violence as "the intentional use of physical force or power, threatened or actual, against oneself, another person, or against a group or community, that either results in or has a high likelihood of resulting in injury, death, [or] psychological harm" (WHO 2002:4). Our ethnographic work focuses attention on *interpersonal* and *collective* violence. The first includes *family* and *intimate partner* violence (i.e., physical aggression "between family members and intimate partners, usually, though not exclusively, taking place in the home" [ibid. 5]) and *community* violence (i.e., physical aggression "between individuals who are unrelated, and who may or may not know each other, generally taking place outside the home" [ibid.]). Our definition of collective violence departs from the WHO's in that it refers to any "episodic social interaction that immediately inflicts physical damage on persons and/or objects ('damage' includes forcible seizure of persons or objects over restraint or resistance), involves at least two perpetrators of damage, and results at least in part from coordination among persons who perform the damaging acts" (Tilly 2003:12). By contrast, the WHO's definition confines collective violence to that inflicted "by larger groups such as states, organized political groups, militia groups and terrorist organizations" (2002:4).

As we will describe below, more encompassing definitions of violence, which include structural and/or symbolic forms (Jackman 2002; Farmer 2004; Bourgois 2009), inspired and informed our perspective on the forms and uses of violence on the ground, but for analytical purposes, we decided to restrict our definition of the phenomenon to the "behavior by persons against persons that intentionally threatens, attempts, or actually inflicts physical harm" (Reiss and Roth 1993:35). There are, in our view, clear analytical advantages of such a circumscribed definition of violence. Paraphrasing the late historian, sociologist, and political scientist Charles Tilly (2003), we could say that spreading the term "violence" across all sorts of relations that we consider unjust, exploitative, or oppressive undermines the effort to explain violence. All-encompassing definitions, in fact, prevent us from asking—as we attempt to do in the pages that follow—about effective causal relationships between structural processes such as informalization, increasing inequality, and/or unlawful state action, on one side, and interpersonal physical damage, on the other.

Daily violence chokes the daily life of the dispossessed with such an overwhelming intensity and frequency that throughout the course of our investigation and writing, we oftentimes wonder how anyone could, to invoke Jaslyn's meditation about her mother's uncertain future in Colum McCann's jarring *Let the Great World Spin*, crawl away from that life and walk away intact. Although the actual long- and medium-term effects of exposure to violence are not the empirical focus of our research (their analysis would have required a very different research design), the area where we conducted our fieldwork is such a hostile terrain to live in that, since the time we decided to focus on violence as the main topic of our research, the main concern—at once scholarly, ethical, and political—underpinning our research and writing revolved around the hard-to-dissipate marks that such a crushing violence is leaving in the hearts, minds, and bodies of those living at the urban margins.[5]

Crime (robberies and homicides) in the area has increased as a result of the informalization of the local economy (informality that, as we will see, takes a very concrete physical form), the growth and expansion of the trade of illicit drugs, and the intermittent, contradictory, and selective presence of the state (in the form of the local police) in the area. The depacification of daily life in Arquitecto Tucci is, in other words, the result of both economic and political processes. One of our self-appointed tasks is to analyze the specific routes by which these processes are making the area more violent. How and why has the growth of an informal market located within the geographic boundaries of the neighborhood increased violence in daily interactions? How does drug dealing feed violence? How does state action amplify interpersonal violence?

Together with this larger explanatory aim, a second task of the book will be to dissect the uses and forms of violence that prevail in the area. Much of the violence under the ethnographic microscope here resembles that which has been dissected by students of street violence in the United States, that is, it is the product of interpersonal retaliation and remains encapsulated in dyadic exchanges (Jacobs 2004; Mullins, Wright, and Jacobs 2004; Jacobs and Wright 2006; Papachristos 2009). An eye for an eye, a tooth for a tooth: in this, the violence in Tucci resembles that which pervades daily life in the most dangerous of US ghettos or inner cities, Brazilian favelas, Colombian *comunas*, and other relegated zones throughout the Americas. However, upon casting a wider net to include other forms of physical aggression (sexual, domestic, and intimate) that take place inside and outside the home, and that intensely shape the course of residents' daily lives, we will begin to see that violence is used for many diverse goals and takes different forms. Violence in the area, we will argue by way of ethnographic demonstration, serves more than just retaliatory purposes, and its many forms often link with one another beyond only dyadic relationships. There are other forms of physical aggression that take place inside poor households and outside in dilapidated streets, and that extend beyond the one-on-one interpersonal interaction acquiring a less clearly delineated, more expansive, form. Violence does not always remain confined to reciprocal exchange, and it sometimes spreads throughout the social fabric of a community, resembling a chain that connects different types of physical harm. Part of our task will be to reconstruct this concatenation of events and show the reader that what looks like an isolated incident is, in fact, part of a larger interactional sequence.

Amid pervasive interpersonal violence, scared residents establish routines and weave relations to cope with (and respond to) the constant danger that besieges them and their beloved ones. In doing so, they exercise what anthropologists Veena Das (2012) and Michael Lambek (2010) call "ordinary ethics." Our third task will be to inspect the ethical routines and practices (some individual, others collective, some violent, others not) that residents of this very dangerous neighborhood use to respond to overwhelming interpersonal violence. Violence, many a social scientific account demonstrates (Anderson 1999; Bourgois 1995; Das 1990; Garbarino 1993), shatters and unravels routine daily existence. But a plethora of "small acts [that] allow life to be knitted pair by pair" (Das 2012:139) also exists (see Villarreal forthcoming). The ethical (here understood as a sense of duty of what is the correct thing to be done, that is, a moral striving [Lambek 2010]) lies precisely there, and our aim will be to locate, unearth, and dissect these "raveling" practices, particularly expressions of care amid a violence that corrodes community life.

According to Tilly, observers of human violence can be divided into three camps: "idea people, behavior people, and relation people" (2003:5). Emphasizing consciousness as the foundation of—and spring for—human action, the first camp claims that

> humans acquire beliefs, concepts, rules, goals, and values from their environments, reshape their own (and each other's) impulses in conformity with such ideas, and act out their socially acquired ideas. . . . [I]deas concerning the worth of others and the desirability of aggressive actions significantly affect the propensity of a person or a people to join in collective violence. To stem violence, goes the reasoning, we must suppress or eliminate destructive ideas. (ibid.)

Behavior people, the second camp, put more stress on "the autonomy of motives, impulses, and opportunities" (ibid. 5–6). While some point toward "human evolution as the origin of aggressive action, individual or collective," others "avoid evolutionary explanations, but still speak of extremely general needs and incentives for domination, exploitation, respect, deference, protection, or security that underlie collective violence. Still others adopt resolutely economistic stances, seeing violence as a means of acquiring goods and services" (ibid. 6). Tilly prefers, and our analysis is inspired and informed by, the third camp: relation people. This perspective makes "transactions among persons and groups far more central than do idea and behavior people" (ibid.). It is through interchanges with other humans— exchanges that always involve some negotiation and creativity— that we develop personalities and practices. For relation people, "ideas thus become means, media, and products of social interchange, while motives, impulses, and opportunities only operate within continuously negotiated social interaction" (ibid.). Taming violence, in this view, "depends less on destroying bad ideas, eliminating opportunities, or suppressing impulses than on transforming relations among persons and groups" (ibid.). We do not deny the existence of ideas and motivations (in fact, we will devote time examining intended "uses" of violence), but, being "relation people," we believe that the first are a product of social interactions and the second always operate in interactive contexts. Accordingly, our analysis of daily violence at the urban margins places analytical emphasis on concatenations and interactions over violent impulses or ideas about violence.

A dispute between dealers over missing payments, like the ones that oftentimes took place during our fieldwork, can be seen as the expression of retaliatory violence—and so can a woman's violent reaction to the assault of her drunkard partner. But when dealers barge into a home, point a gun at the face of the mother of an addict, and claim a drug payment, and when this same mother threatens to "break the fingers" of her addicted son (or, actually, punches him until she sees "blood coming out of his face," or calls the cops she knows are involved in drug trafficking to have her son arrested and taken away) in order to prevent him from stealing things from her house (things like a small TV set that he then sells to finance his addiction) that do not belong to his mother but to her second husband who, enraged by the missing items, often beats her— then we are confronting concatenated violent exchanges, and we need to move beyond one-on-one retaliation to better understand what violence is about. Rather than "telling" about violent interactions and concatenations, we will, following the very best of the now reborn ethnographic tradition in sociology, privilege the "ethnographic showing" (for exemplars, see Desmond 2007; Comfort 2008; Contreras 2012; Goffman 2014). Rather than simply asserting that different types of violence are connected, we want the reader to be able to see, through our ethnographic material, how these concatenations operate in the real time and space of a relegated urban area.

The ethnographic vignettes below will show the many interconnections between diverse deployments of violence. We were there, as observant participants in the school, in the homes, in the streets, and in the communal soup kitchen, and we are now here, attempting what, to paraphrase anthropologist Nancy Scheper-Hughes, we call a "good enough reconstruction" of what we saw, heard, and witnessed. This showing rather than telling is crucial, we believe, in order to abuse neither our authority as writers nor the readers' trust.

If we are to avoid misleading and stigmatizing interpretations of what violence at the urban margins is all about, then context is crucial. In order to understand and explain violent concatenations, we need to engage in what Carol Heimer calls "radical contextualization" (1988). Part of the analytical reconstruction of each selected episode involves its placement in its larger structural context and in its most immediate situational one. This, we also know, is easier said than done. When attempting to understand each violent interaction, we struggled hard, as American novelist Richard Ford so eloquently put it, to simultaneously hold in the mind the objective and subjective contexts, "one so close to the other . . . as two sides of" that "one thing" we call violence. Given that we will present the ethnographic material in its full detail, the reader should be able to judge whether or not we succeeded in the attempt.

Without an understanding of the ways in which those involved in violence make sense of it (how they use it, experience it, and what they try to accomplish with it), we would be left with a rather limited and limiting examination of violence as simply caused by macrostructural forces. True, "big structures" and "large processes"—in our case, a patriarchal state that engages in illegal practices, the vast informalization of the economy, and the growth of illicit drug trade—are key factors in the perpetuation of some forms of violence and the increase of others. But an account of large-scale structures and processes is not enough to understand and explain the diverse (and interconnected) forms of interpersonal brutality found on the ground. In order to do so, we need to reconstruct the perspectives of those who as victims, perpetrators, and/or witnesses (roles that, as we will see, are always in flux) are within this maelstrom of multiple and oftentimes vicious forms of physical aggression. Reconstructing and explaining (or, in Pierre Bourdieu's perspective, "understanding") the "locals' points of view" as they *are expressed in the course of daily interaction*—still a defining feature of "good enough" ethnographic research—should thus complement and enrich our analysis of the objective context of violence. We emphasize reconstruction and explanation because, as Annick Prieur reminded us a while ago, it is still "necessary and valuable . . . to try to understand a culture in the way the participants understand it themselves, to take on their point of view—to *dare* to take on their point of view—regardless of how politically and morally incorrect it may be"(1998:21, her emphasis). But if we are to move beyond a mere "collection of personal testimonies," we need to "try to understand why their perception is the way it is." And for this, again, contexts are crucial.

By the end of this book, the reader will not know why this or that neighbor beats his or her child, why this or that husband punches his wife, why this or that youngster robs a neighbor at gunpoint, or why this or that resident shoots at another one. But she or he will understand how and why violence in the Arquitecto Tucci neighborhood is a *routine way of dealing with everyday life issues inside and outside the home*. In other words, the reader will be able to understand how and why physical aggression is part of the local *repertoire of action*—a habitual way of acting on individual and collective interests.[6] The reader will thus be able to make sense of residents' reliance on violence to address individual and collective problems (from disciplining a misbehaving child to establishing authority in the neighborhood or at home). Considering violence as part of a repertoire, as we do here, does not mean that all of the residents in the relegated urban area under consideration resort to violence as a way of solving daily problems—in the same sense that the existence of a repertoire of collective action does not mean that all citizens participate in a particular form of joint action (Tilly 1986; 1995). Approaching violence as an element within a repertoire, on the contrary, means that violence is an established "know-how," a familiar practice that is useful in dealing with the difficulties that daily life presents at the urban margins (a rape threat, a robbery, an "out-of-control" child, etc.).

At first sight, many of the episodes we will present throughout the book might look like cruel actions. In other words, they may seem to be driven by the intention of imposing pain on a weaker human being with the exclusive aim of causing angst or fear, that is, pure and simple "cruelty" (Shklar 1985). However, the violent acts that seem to have one end (e.g., to humiliate and/or frighten) have, in fact, another one—an aim that reveals itself after careful and sustained scrutiny. Let's *listen* to the mother who stops beating her child only after she sees blood coming out of her own hands, or to another one who chains her daughter to the bed (or whips her with a stick). She describes in detail the mechanics of violence—the form in which she punches, the marks left on her and her loved ones' bodies—but also the frustration and impotence that lead to those hurting movements. If we keep listening, and if we attempt to take her point of view—again, if we *dare* to take her point of view—we will see that the ultimate aim of that violence over a weaker being is not to instill fear in the victim (in which case we could, in effect, call it a "cruel" action). The production of fear is, from the point of view of the perpetrator, a means to prevent a greater evil (as we will see, this can take the form of "bad company," "drug addiction," etc.), a way of solving (or attempting to solve) a pressing, urgent problem. As experienced by many a perpetrator, violence is oftentimes seen as an attempt to break a very dangerous sequence of events (which, as we will see, takes the following form for most residents: drugs → robbery → death or prison). By the book's end we hope the reader will understand that what from the outside looking in gives the impression of an exercise of cruelty is from the inside looking out part of a repertoire that *makes sense* only if we carefully consider the circumstances under which it operates.

A NOTE ON METHOD: A SOCIOLOGIST AND AN ELEMENTARY SCHOOLTEACHER JOIN FORCES

This book is a product of the collaboration between an elementary schoolteacher who has worked in the area since 2003 and a sociologist who first came to the neighborhood twenty-five years ago (when he was a political party activist), and who returned there, intermittently as a researcher, between 2009 and 2012. The book is based on the analysis of field notes written by the teacher at the end of each working day (she worked in three different schools in the area during the time of our fieldwork) and of in-depth interviews conducted with dozens of residents, with doctors who work at the local hospital and health center, with police agents who work at the local precinct, and with school personnel. The analysis also draws upon material collected during focus groups organized with local high school students, pictures taken by elementary schoolchildren as part of a photography workshop we organized at the local school, and drawings made by students on what they perceive to be positive and negative aspects of their neighborhood. The book is also based on the analysis of official records and newspaper reports, and on one hundred short interviews that sought to identify residential patterns, sources of employment, levels of education, and the most common problems identified by the population under investigation.[7] During 2010 and 2011, Agustín Burbano de Lara (then a sociology senior at the University of Buenos Aires) joined our research team and conducted observations and in-depth interviews at one of the local soup kitchens. We use some of the stories that Agustín collected during six months of intensive and demanding fieldwork—properly noticing when they come from his own ethnographic immersion. The methodological appendix provides further detail on the data production techniques that went into the makings of this book.

We did not begin our fieldwork with the intention of capturing violence in real time and space. Field research started as an attempt to replicate the study of "environmental suffering" that one of us, together with a "native anthropologist," had carried out in a highly contaminated shantytown neighborhood named Flammable (Auyero and Swistun 2009). We wanted to know how contamination was experienced when its sources were not as visible as in Flammable, a neighborhood that sits adjacent to a very large petrochemical compound. Only a few weeks into our research, the local school students began to bring us—together with "toxic stories" (the open-air garbage dumps, the rats that were "all over," the "potable" water that tastes like oil)—accounts of murders, rapes, shootings, and domestic fights. When we asked them to draw the things they liked in their neighborhood and the things they disliked, they came back with the quite graphic illustrations that we present in chapter 2: sketches where interpersonal violence has prominent presence. As a result of this initial—quite unexpected—encounter with local viewpoints, we decided to shift the empirical focus of our investigation.

At the beginning, we did not know how to approach our main subject. We were, to be frank, quite astonished. Our daily records of violence(s) of shootings, fights, and so on ran parallel to our somewhat frantic readings of scholarship on the topic—reading that, both in sociology and psychology, tends to treat different forms of violence (domestic, sexual, street, drug-related) as distinct and discrete phenomena. That is why, at the beginning of our fieldwork, we tried to understand a dispute inside the home as an interaction divorced from, say, a shooting between drug dealers—and there are very good scholarly reasons to preserve the analytic distinction between these different types. The case of an attempted rape of a young girl followed by a beating perpetrated by a group of neighbors on the presumed sexual predator alerted us to the possible connections between forms of violence that, in our records, appear disassociated. Slowly, we began to construct a different object of research—not one focused on the individual acts of violence but on their concatenations.

A few months into our fieldwork, one of us wrote the following field note:

> August 20, 2009. Victor, my student (ten years old), tells me that yesterday, a "kid was killed" close to his home. "It was a band of thieves, or maybe they were drug dealers." Another student, Samantha (nine) says that she was on the sidewalk when she heard the shooting. Moved and scared, I tell them to be careful. In unison, Samantha and Victor reply, "Oh, don't worry teacher, we are used to it."

Since we recorded this note, we not only began to expand the scope of our investigation (to include diverse forms of violence such as domestic and sexual, and to analyze the way in which they link with one another and with more "public" ones, in the street and in the household) but also attempted to excavate deeper in order to examine both violent interactions and the "hearts and minds"—that is, the subjectivities—of those who perpetrate and suffer them.

ON THE ROAD AHEAD: THEORY, POINTILLISM, AND PARADOXES

Observations, formal interviews, informal conversations, newspaper reports, and official records collected during thirty months of team fieldwork point to interpersonal violence in the area as what anthropologist Marcel Mauss (1966) would call a "total social fact," that is, a relational activity that not only has deeper roots in (and larger implications throughout) society but that is at once *economic*, *political*, and *ethical*, private and public, individual and collective. The chapters that follow will examine all these different dimensions of violence and place them under the ethnographic microscope.

Chapter 1 begins with a general description of the extreme levels of material deprivation and the meager forms of palliative state assistance that characterize daily life in the neighborhood where we conducted our fieldwork. We examine the neighborhood's recent history as one marked by deindustrialization and informalization—both processes driven by the great neoliberal transformation that the country as a whole went through in the last forty years. We then examine the formation and pacification of the informal street market known as La Salada (an important source of jobs for the local population), and the depacification of its surrounding area. We delve into the twenty-year history and current operation of La Salada in order to examine the role violence played in the origins of the market, and the ways in which the daily functioning of the market has, over time, become more "civilized" (i.e., devoid of violence, as in the sense used by Norbert Elias [1978; 1994]). Here we pay particular attention to the role played by managers and enforcers in concentrating the means of violence and extraction. Drawing upon available crime data, interviews with primary informants, and ethnographic fieldwork, the last section of this chapter scrutinizes the increasing levels of interpersonal violence in the area adjacent to the market as the result of expanding opportunities for crime.

Not all the violence that shakes poor people's lives in Arquitecto Tucci is opportunistic, tied to the operation of the informal market, or confined to retaliatory dyadic relationships. Chapter 2 begins with a series of ethnographic descriptions of the different types of violence that coexist in the neighborhood and sometimes overlap in the everyday life of its residents. After a summary treatment of the different ways in which social science has approached the issue of interpersonal violence, we engage in a series of ethnographic reconstructions that depict the concatenations of different types of intentional perpetration of physical harm.

When confronted with such levels of interpersonal violence, political sociology is compelled to ask how the state polices poor people's disputes. Such is the task of chapter 3, where we examine the intermittent, skewed, and contradictory character of state presence at the urban margins. We pay particular attention to the role of the local police in the area and the way it partakes in the crime it is supposed to be controlling and also reveal the deeply political character of violence in the area.

In chapter 4 we further scrutinize this political dimension by exploring the forms of collective action that it engenders, and the paradoxical forms of informal social control that rely on state agents as key actors. We also explore the ethical dimension of violence by examining the practices and routines residents engage in to protect themselves and their loved ones. In the conclusion, we draw upon the main findings presented in each chapter and establish parallels and convergences with other territories of urban relegation in the Americas in order to sketch the outline of a political sociology of urban marginality. Overall, our reconstruction reveals the somewhat equivocal character of violence in the area. Violence dislocates individuals' lives and disrupts the collective life of the neighborhood. But acts of aggression and the fearful responses they generate also provide some sort of (albeit, partial and transitory) order— a momentary oasis of peaceful truce in the midst of a concatenation of violent events. As we will see in the case of the informal market, violence also gives birth to (more lasting) stability—upon which nonviolent transactions are able to take place and expand.

With the exception of a brief description of the different ways in which interpersonal violence has been understood and explained in academic literature, the reader will find neither detailed analytic recipes nor large theoretical proclamations. In our view, the best proof of a useful theorization and of an adequate recipe (and of a careful reading of extant scholarship) does not lie in a chapter that describes the "frame" of the research but in the actual utilization of these theoretical and analytical tools. Theory for us is, indeed, a tool box. The stories we present below were reconstructed with a set of analytic and theoretical concerns in mind (about the origins, forms, and effects of interpersonal violence). In other words, we made theoretically informed choices regarding what story to present and what aspects of it to emphasize. These stories are not—despite possible appearances to the contrary—stories of individuals but of violence. Different perspectives guided the construction of our sociological object, but we decided, both for readability and for convictions about the ways in which theory should be mobilized, to embed these different scholarly approaches in our analysis—as opposed to the usual style that divorces theory from description and interpretation in the (sadly, still present) form of a (usually overtheorized) frame filled with "authority citations" and subsequent "empirical section."

While we seek to extend and refine (Burawoy 1991) a set of theories about interpersonal violence without falling into the scholastic trap of overtheorization, our tight focus on violent interpersonal interactions runs what we could call the "risk of pointillism"[8]—a hazard that regularly affects ethnographic research. A technique of painting, in which tiny dots of primary colors (our meticulous reconstructions of violent interactions) are used in patterns to create an image (in our case, violence at the urban margins), a pointillist ethnography of violence should not lose sight of what lies at the root of the increase of some forms of violence and the persistence of others. In order to avoid this risk, much of the narrative that follows goes back and forth between what anthropologist Clifford Geertz (1973) aptly termed the "small facts" and the "larger issues" while—and herein lies the greatest "Seuratian" challenge—making sure that the connections between them are clearly specified. Some chapters emphasize more detailed reconstructions while others provide broader parameters. Hopefully, by the end of this book, the reader will have a good sense of the general picture, that is, the processes and mechanisms that structure violence at the margins from outside the specific harmful interactions.

Violence lives a double life. It leads one life in the objectivity of murder rates, the numbers of injuries and surgeries, and the geographical locations of physical attacks (inside the home, in the street, in this or that area of the neighborhood). It lives another life in the subjectivities of victims, perpetrators, and witnesses—in the experience of violence and the meanings assigned to it. A social scientific approach to violence should thus exert a double reading, attentive to its objective and subjective dimensions but keenly aware of the fact that violence, paraphrasing Émile Durkheim, must ultimately be explained not by the conceptions of it created by those who participate in it (as important as these conceptions are), but by the profound causes that oftentimes escape their awareness. In order to do so—that is, in order to engage in a double reading that, attentive to the dots, does not lose sight of the larger picture—the focus of our sociological analysis will be on both relations and interactions: not on violent "individuals" or "institutions" but on many types of *relations* (between the space of the neighborhood and the larger social structure, between the neighborhood and the adjacent informal market, and between the neighborhood and the state) and *interactions* (between partners inside and outside the household, residents in and out of the streets, neighbors and police agents, etc.). The violence of these interactions, we believe, can only be understood and explained with the larger economic and political dynamics in mind. Otherwise, there will just be dots. In other words, although our focus will be on the interactional concatenation of violence, we should not lose sight of the historical chain of events that have led to the present moment. In chapter 1 we precisely seek to bring this history to the foreground. The everyday structuring of violent concatenations explored in the ethnographic chapters is intimately linked with the historical structure examined in this chapter—concatenations and depacification are mutually imbricated. We ask the reader to keep this in mind because it will enhance our understanding of both the chronic uncertainty within which Tucci residents live and the repertoire that emerges from (and sustains) it.

The bulk of this book focuses on what residents in Arquitecto Tucci do, think, and feel about violence—and on the enigmas and paradoxes that these practices, beliefs, and feelings present to us. When a woman grabs an apple with her hands, breaks it into two halves, and states that it was "just like this . . . practicing with the apple," that she learned what she calls "killing techniques," and then adds that her grandfather "taught her self-defense" to protect herself from her brothers, the story will alert us to the "learned" character of violence. When a ten-year-old boy shows us his new cell phone and tells us that his father, a police agent, gave it to him as a present after having taken it from a thief, or when a dealer describes her agreements with the local police, these stories make us reflect on the presence of the state in the area. When mothers of neighborhood adolescents resort to a police force they distrust to discipline their sons and daughters, a detailed description of how this happens leads us to unveil a "voluntary" involvement in forms of state control. A thorough reconstruction of a domestic fight that occurred after a dispute over drugs, in turn, shows us the way to think about and closely examine the possible concatenations of different types of violence. Thus, what might look like "tiny dots" in the pointillist analogy—or "simply anecdotes" in the criticism often launched against ethnographic evidence—are, in fact, analytical reconstructions whose purpose is to offer a good enough understanding and explanation of the dynamics of interpersonal violence at the urban margins.

CHAPTER 1

EL BARRIO AND LA FERIA
DAILY LIFE AT THE URBAN MARGINS

Arquitecto Tucci (pop. 170,000) sits in the southern part of metropolitan Buenos Aires. It is located adjacent to the banks of the highly polluted Riachuelo River—"the worst ecological disaster of the country," according to the Federal Ombudsman.[1] Extreme levels of infrastructural deprivation—or what Bruce Braun and James McCarthy (2005) would term the material dimension of state abandonment—characterize the area: unpaved streets, open-air sewers, broken sidewalks, scarce lighting, and random garbage collection (figures 3 and 4). Levels of poverty (as measured by unsatisfied basic needs and by income) are more than double the average of the state.

Three different urban forms coexist in contemporary Arquitecto Tucci: the traditional working-class neighborhood, shantytowns, and squatter settlements. The most recent squatter settlement (informally known as "el campito") was formed five years ago and is experiencing rapid vertical expansion. This area is more prone to flooding (during our fieldwork we oftentimes witnessed new residents leveling their plots with garbage and waste—quite likely toxic—extracted from the Riachuelo). While the streets and blocks in the older part of the

FIGURE 3. The neighborhood: The rough ground.

FIGURE 4. The neighborhood: The rough ground.

neighborhood and in the squatter settlement follow the pattern of urban zoning (known as the *forma damero* or checkerboard form), the shantytown's winding alleyways and passages do not. Residents in the older neighborhood are property owners and generally better off compared to shantytown dwellers and squatters, both of whom have still-unresolved land tenure issues (lack of security that often becomes a source of conflict: "when neighbors want to grab a piece of our land, my dad shoots at them").

The pictures in figures 5–13 were taken by the students of the local school as part of a photography workshop we organized with them during 2011. They portray, with particular clarity, widespread infrastructural deprivation (Rodgers and O'Neill 2012) and the vast array of risks residents are exposed to on a daily basis—and that determine high levels of what in other work one of us labeled "environmental suffering" (Auyero and Swistun 2009). One of Fernanda's early notes illustrates this point:

FIGURE 5. Infrastructural deprivation.

June 9, 2010: Manuel's mother came to see me. Manuel is my student and has been absent for many days. She tells me that Manuel is full of pimples—just like her eight other children . . . They live along the [highly contaminated] banks of [a dead river known as] the Riachuelo.

FIGURE 6. Uncollected garbage.

FIGURE 7. Putrid waters. "It's all filled with garbage."

In the vast majority of the more than three hundred photos taken by students, garbage, odor, and the discomfort generated by them are a constant presence. On several occasions students point their blaming fingers at neighbors, whom they see as responsible for dumping. But, at the same time, they emphasize

FIGURE 8. Mud in the streets.

FIGURE 9. "I like these streets. They are paved."

that the irregular garbage collection is the main reason why they throw their waste into the streets or in the nearby stream.

The contrast between the many dirt roads (which, as we saw on more than one occasion, force children to wrap their only pair of shoes with plastic bags because "when it rains, it's all

FIGURE 10. Mud in the streets.

FIGURE 11. The playground.

FIGURE 12. "It's ugly. The street is broken; buses cannot go through."

FIGURE 13. "The car was burned down . . . It's filled with garbage."

muddy and you sink in the street") and the few paved roads was also a recurring theme in the photos. The "completely rotten" water stream, and the garbage that accumulates there, were other issues repeatedly emphasized. In one conversation that emerged from these photos, several students told us they had seen the mud—highly contaminated with all kinds of toxins dredged from the Riachuelo—deposited in the land of new squatter settlements and used for land leveling.[2] Many pictures combine students' distaste for the lack of basic infrastructure with straightforward depictions of the prevalence of crime and drug problems: drug selling points, stolen (and then burned) cars, and so on.

Because participants in the photography workshop were told to portray the space of the neighborhood, they did not take photos inside the school. But extreme relegation—in the literal sense of "demotion" or "oblivion"—is also prevalent there. The water treatment plant that sits adjacent to the school oftentimes ceases to work, flooding the school yard and sending its pungent smell inside the classrooms. As Fernanda wrote in one of her many field notes on the subject:

> May 11, 2010: Today, the smell from the water treatment plant is unbearable. We can't open the window of the classroom because we are right in front of it. During lunchtime, the kids don't want to eat. They tell me: "It's really disgusting to eat with this odor." The plant has been malfunctioning for the last seventeen years.

The school building is also in quite poor shape. As Fernanda notes:

> May 15, 2010: In order to go to the cafeteria to have breakfast, we now need to go through the outside patio because the covered patio is closed. The roof there is about to fall off.

> August 3, 2010: I arrive at school at 7:30 a.m. and the principal tells me that part of the ceiling in the main area of the school fell off. This part of the school is now closed. The other area, which was closed months ago, has not yet been repaired.

Dozens of pages of Fernanda's diary attest to the sad and simple fact that children in Buenos Aires neighborhoods of relegation attend relegated schools that warehouse future generations while hardly acting as bulwarks against the dangers of daily life. Anybody who spends a few days in either of the schools where she works would have trouble recognizing them as educational institutions. Between 8:00 a.m. and noon, two full hours are spent serving breakfast, lunch, and two breaks; as a consequence, students receive an average of one hundred minutes of effective class time per day. During 2009, students never had a full week of classes; classes were canceled once or twice every week either because teachers or auxiliary personnel were on strike, demanding better working conditions and/or salary increases, or because of malfunctioning buildings. In both schools, the average student had three days of classes per week.

Despite the images and accompanying testimonies, it would be wrong to conclude that the state has entirely deserted Arquitecto Tucci. One public hospital, one new public urgent care unit (Unidad de Pronta Atención [UPA]), several public schools, the Asignación Universal por Hijo (the largest Argentine conditional cash transfer program, effective since 2008), and many other welfare programs (e.g., Argentina Trabaja, Plan Vida) mark the state's presence in the area and provide assistance to most of its residents. A little more than half of our one hundred short interviewees (54 percent) benefit from one or more of these state programs. Patronage networks linked to the governing party and soup kitchens funded by Catholic charities provide other crucial resources, such as food and medicine, for the residents. Finally, the informal labor market contributes to many household incomes in the area. Construction, domestic service, and scavenging are the occupations most frequently reported by the local population.

After a decade of sustained record levels of economic growth in Argentina, Arquitecto Tucci continues to be a marginalized space characterized by crumbling infrastructure, dysfunctional institutions, and all sorts of environmental hazards. It is inhabited by masses of informal workers and unemployed individuals who barely make ends meet. Borrowing from urban theorist Mike Davis, Tucci is "a sink for surplus labour which can only keep pace with subsistence by ever more heroic feats of self-exploitation and the further competitive subdivision of already densely filled survival niches" (2006:27). From Fernanda's field diary:

> May 6, 2010: As I am entering the school building, Luis's mother comes to talk to me. Luis has not been in school for at least a month. She tells me they've been living in the street, sleeping in a kind of storage space. They were allowed to stay there until 5:00 a.m. Then they would start scavenging the streets and asking for food in restaurants and bars. They are now renting a house in a nearby barrio. They are all from the province of Formosa. . . . She begins to cry as she tells me her story. She tells me that she was very scared while sleeping on the streets. She is worried for Luis; she doesn't want him to miss more classes. Luis's face is full of scars.

Together with state assistance, charity aid, and informal jobs, the other main source of subsistence for the population is the largest street fair in the country, located at the neighborhood's northern limit. Known by the name La Salada, the fair consists of three different markets where, twice a week, thousands of shoppers buy counterfeit apparel, small electronics, and food.[3] Founded at the beginning of the 1990s, La Salada has been declared a "world emblem of illegal commerce" by the European Union for the enormous quantity of *mercadería falsificada* (counterfeit merchandise) one finds there.[4] Either as owners, or, more likely, as employees of one of the fair's thousands of stalls (7,822 according to one recent reliable count [Dewey 2014]), or as highly exploited workers in one of the hundreds of sweatshops that manufacture the goods sold there, many residents' economic subsistence is tied to this vast street fair. Twenty-two percent of our one hundred interviewees regularly work in La Salada, and so do many of the elementary schoolchildren and high school students who, given that the feria operates through the night, miss school classes twice a week. The sphere of influence of this informal market extends well beyond those who directly work there: elementary schoolchildren, for example, work as babysitters for the women who work in the sweatshops that supply La Salada or who spend long hours through the night at one of the feria's stands. As Rocio (ten) tells us while describing the picture she took for the workshop: "I took a picture of the sewing machine. It's in a warehouse behind the train tracks. A woman works there, and I take care of her daughter while she sews. She works for a guy who works at the feria. With what she pays me, I buy food for home or clothes for myself."

In what follows, we present the sixty-year history of Arquitecto Tucci as one of *deindustrialization* and *informalization*. Both processes, we argue, were driven by the neoliberalization of the economy that began in the mid-1970s and accelerated in the early 1990s. We then delve into the twenty-year history and current operation of La Salada in order to examine the role violence played in the origins of the market, and the ways in which the daily functioning of the market has, over time, become more "civilized" (i.e., devoid of violence). Based on archival and secondary sources, we pay particular attention to the role played by managers and enforcers in concentrating the means of violence and extraction. We argue, by way of empirical demonstration, that the pacification of the market—that is, *its civilization*—is the result of the successful efforts of a small group of entrepreneurial street vendors-turned-administrators to monopolize (a) the use of force inside the market, and (b) the extraction of informal taxes from other vendors. Through this dual monopolization of force and tax extraction, organizations with state-like properties emerged within the market that contributed to its pacification and fostered its expansion. As the market consolidated and gained popularity, however, opportunities for crime multiplied and levels of interpersonal violence increased in the surrounding areas. Drawing upon available crime data, interviews with primary informants, and ethnographic fieldwork, the last section of this chapter scrutinizes the increasing levels of interpersonal violence in the area adjacent to the market as the result of expanding opportunities for crime and sets the stage for the analysis of different forms of violence prevailing in the neighborhood.[5]

ARQUITECTO TUCCI IN HISTORICAL CONTEXT: FROM INDUSTRIAL TO INFORMAL SUBURBS

In the early 1930s, Argentina embarked on a process of import substitution industrialization that had as its epicenter the city of Buenos Aires and its surrounding metropolitan area. The growth of manufacturing, and the reduction of the agricultural sector in the pampas and in the rest of the interior, fostered massive internal migration from rural areas in Argentina to Buenos Aires, and the subsequent *proletarianization* of the new urban industrial working classes. As historian David Rock synthesizes, "Between the triennial averages of 1927–1929 and 1941–1943, manufacturing grew at an annual rate of 3.4 percent, as against only 1.5 percent in the rural sector and 1.8 in gross domestic product. Imports of manufactured consumer goods, around 40 percent of total imports before 1930, had fallen to less than 25 percent by the late 1940s" (1987:232). Wartime interruptions in foreign trade had caused a general decline in the level of agricultural exports since the mid-1930s. While unemployment was escalating in the countryside, industrial workers in the outskirts of Buenos Aires multiplied.

Proletarianization went hand in hand with the suburbanization of the newly arrived migrants-turned-industrial workers. In striking contrast to the historical pattern found in the United States (Fishman 1989), the main actors of the first wave of suburbanization in Buenos Aires were the urban poor and working classes (Torres 1990). Between 1937 and 1947, nearly 750,000 internal migrants arrived in Greater Buenos Aires (GBA) or the Conurbano Bonaerense (as said before, the commonly known name for the metropolitan area comprised of thirty-three municipal districts surrounding the city of Buenos Aires). Economic crisis in the countryside "pushed" while employment opportunities and much better wages in Buenos Aires "pulled" many countrymen to Buenos Aires (Rock 1987).

In the years that followed this first wave of massive internal migration, the annual rate of migration to GBA from the country continued to increase. In 1947, 4.7 million people were living in GBA. Thirteen years later, almost 7 million resided in a considerable number of new suburban settlements: working-class neighborhoods (barrios) and slums or shantytowns (*villas*) in suburbs of the city like Avellaneda, Lanús, and Lomas de Zamora, where Arquitecto Tucci is located. The state-owned railway system and state-subsidized bus lines bolstered this suburbanization of low-income groups during the 1940s and 1950s—the train connected previously inaccessible areas to the city of Buenos Aires, and the many bus lines connected train stations with newly opened residential areas.[6]

Starting in the 1940s and 1950s, Arquitecto Tucci became home to thousands of these new migrants who found jobs in nearby plants (metallurgic, meatpacking, and textile). As standard housing was scarce and extremely expensive for the low income levels of the new migrants-becoming-industrial-proletarians, deserted lands around the city and close to newly installed factories became natural squatting grounds for thousands of migrant families. Most of this land, such as present-day Arquitecto Tucci, was located on the flood plain of the Matanza/Riachuelo/Reconquista river basin. For newcomers to the city, the "bridgeheaders," as Alejandro Portes calls them, "occupation, and not housing, is the paramount consideration" (1972:279). Over the years, and through what Peter Ward (Ward et al. 2011) calls self-help housing (i.e., *autoconstrucción*), they would slowly build their own homes.

Fast-forward from the 1970s to 2010. With solid brick homes and paved streets, the area where the first inhabitants of Arquitecto Tucci established themselves looks nothing like the original settlement. However, the new residential areas surrounding the old neighborhood (many of them lowlands squatted by new migrants or by the descendants of the older residents) are, as noted above, still characterized by extreme levels of infrastructural deprivation.

But the most striking transformation in Arquitecto Tucci is the disappearance of formal work and the impressive informalization of its working population. Blue-collar workers of the kind that first inhabited Arquitecto Tucci fifty years ago are no longer found among the approximately 170,000 that live there today. These days the informal labor market is the mainstay of subsistence for households in the area. At the root of this change is what we could call, paraphrasing Karl Polanyi, the great neoliberal transformation that took place in Argentina from the mid-1970s until the early 2000s.

Although many of the economic changes brought about by the military dictatorship of 1976–83 had neoliberal features, the main period of neoliberalization—as a political "vehicle for the restoration of class power" (Harvey 2005)—took place in the early 1990s and had the following main characteristics: financial deregulation, privatization, flexibilization of labor markets, and trade liberalization (Teubal 2004; Cooney 2007). During the first half of the 1990s, the "swift and thorough" (Teubal 2004:181) neoliberal experiment in Argentina generated high rates of economic growth (though decoupled from employment generation) and monetary stability. The longer-term result, however, was a second deep wave of deindustrialization (the first one took place during the military dictatorship) and an attendant deproletarianization, which resulted in a "growing heterogeneous mass of unemployed people without institutional protection from either the state, the unions, or other organizations" (Villalón 2007:140).

The disappearance of formal manufacturing jobs came with the growth of informal employment. As economist Paul Cooney states, "Informal work in Buenos Aires and surroundings (Gran Buenos Aires) grew to reach 38 percent of all employment by 1999, and such jobs are estimated to have incomes 45 percent lower than formal employment" (2007:24). Thus, from the early 1990s until the early 2000s, the impoverishment of the middle- and low-income sectors was driven by the disappearance of formal work and an explosion in unemployment levels. In this, the Argentine experience with neoliberalism, despite being "extreme" (Teubal 2004), was unexceptional; as elsewhere, it resulted in "a fall in popular consumption, a deterioration of social conditions, a rise in poverty, immiseration and insecurity, heightened inequalities, social polarization, and resultant political conflict" (Robinson 2008:20; see also Arondskin 2001; Altimir et al. 2002). The crisis and popular uprising of 2001 further dramatized the effects of this great neoliberal transformation (see Auyero 2007 and Levey, Ozarow, and Wylde 2014 for an analysis of mass discontent and the ensuing riots).

Since 2003, poverty rates seem to be declining.[7] The GDP has been growing at an annual rate of 9 percent, and unemployment and poverty rates have decreased to their mid-1990s levels. And yet, 34 percent of the total population lives below the poverty line, and 12 percent subsists under the indigence line (Salvia 2007:28). Even after the economic recovery that began in 2003, poor people's material and symbolic conditions were deeply affected by the sustained decline of income levels in the lower rungs of the job market and the growth of informal employment. In a detailed empirical analysis of recent socioeconomic indicators, sociologist Agustín Salvia argues that since 2003, "economic growth, increase in domestic spending, increment in the aggregate demand of jobs, improvement in formal workers' income, expansion in social assistance programs, and reduction of indigence and poverty (as measured by income) . . . [these processes] have not reduced the inequalities originated in the segmentation of the labor market and in the population's structural living conditions" (2013:2). In fact, Salvia argues persuasively, inequalities have increased and "crystallized." In other words, more than a decade of economic growth has failed to address the "problems of structural marginality that affect at least one in four Argentines" (decent employment, housing, health, and educational services) (ibid.). This segment of the population can only count on the "state's social assistance in the form of conditional cash transfer programs" that provide no way out of their "structural exclusion" (ibid. 30–31).

Arquitecto Tucci is *similar* to many poor neighborhoods in Greater Buenos Aires in that, as noted, its working population now survives through a combination of informal jobs and state assistance (in the form, as said above, of the conditional cash transfer program Asignación Universal por Hijo and other welfare programs). Arquitecto Tucci is *different* from other poverty enclaves in that it is the site of the largest street market in the country, La Salada (figures 14–16), to which we now turn.

LA SALADA

No one debates the sheer magnitude of La Salada, yet conclusive numbers on its scale and impact remain elusive. By cautious estimates, the market receives 50,000 shoppers each day it opens (Girón 2011:33). Customers come not only from Buenos Aires but from throughout Argentina, as well as neighboring countries, to shop not just for themselves but, more often, to buy merchandise wholesale to then resell in as many locales as from which they came (Girón 2011; Pogliaghi 2008). They come to shop at between 7,800 (Dewey 2014) and 30,000 (Girón 2011) stalls and buy from, according to Leticia Pogliaghi (2008), anywhere between 20,000 and 30,000 merchants. Guides even provide shopping tours of La Salada. While clothing and related merchandise is the central attraction at La Salada ("95 percent of stallholders sell garments including T-shirts, jeans, jackets, shoes, socks, underwear, children's clothing, and aprons" [Dewey 2014:10]), individuals working there also make ends meet by selling CDs and food, working as security, running parking lots, or even operating gambling tables. Those working at La Salada are mostly Bolivians and Argentines; almost no one has received formal educational training in business or management, while only a few have any previous experience

FIGURE 14. La Salada at night. Photo credit: Subcoop.

in such activities (Pogliaghi 2008:78). In annual sales, according to journalist Nacho Girón (2011:277), the feria makes around 16 billion pesos (in 2011 currency, about $4 billion)—a staggering amount, as even the most lucrative shopping centers fail to

FIGURE 15. Interior of La Salada at night. Photo credit: Sarah Pabst.

FIGURE 16. Selling in La Salada. Photo credit: Sarah Pabst.

bring in more than 2 billion pesos (about $0.5 billion) a year. Incredibly, in fitting with the informal nature of the market, all transactions at La Salada take place in cash—outside the purview of banks or the state, without checks or credit cards. Yet, in spite of this, the majority of those working at La Salada are at the subsistence level (Pogliaghi 2008:77).

The history of the plots of land in Arquitecto Tucci that were to become La Salada follow, in their own peculiar ways, the larger shifts seen in the nation's economic and demographic structure—as documented above—over the last half century. Before unchecked industrialization transformed the area and the adjacent Riachuelo River into the icons of state neglect and contamination that they are today, it was a zone of natural pools and health resorts. In those days the salty waters of the area were understood to have important health benefits, and the plots of land held successful pools where people would get away, relax, and have picnic gatherings. But, by the 1970s, it became easier for people to travel to the coast, which challenged and thus diminished La Salada's popularity as a vacation spot. In the 1980s, unions began purchasing their own resort clubs and providing workers free access, which only further undermined the need for private pools and health clubs like those offered in Arquitecto Tucci (Girón 2011:42). The final blow came in the 1990s, as an owner of one such pool recounts: "the economic situation was terrible. Menem [president of Argentina 1989–99] destroyed everything. There was no money to eat, how would there be money to go to the pool?" (ibid.). Yet larger shifts in the state and economy negatively impacted the zone in even more ways. Manuel Presa, the owner of Punta Mogote, a resort club that later became home to the most successful fair at La Salada, explains: "The neglect of the area was fundamental; the filthiness of the Riachuelo [River], the open-air landfills, the shantytowns, the increase in the crime rate. It was impossible for people to do tourism and recreation in a place so fallen apart" (ibid. 43). While the pools were later filled, as part of the "public works" infrastructural projects born with the emergence of state-like organizations at La Salada, some of the fairs—including Punta Mogote—still bear the names of those old popular pool resorts (Pogliaghi 2008:42).

Around 1991, a group of roughly one hundred Bolivian street vendors arrived at what would become La Salada (Girón 2011:29). They came to Arquitecto Tucci only after having lived a history of setting up their street markets in different places throughout Buenos Aires, always to eventually be pushed out by the police and their demands for ever-increasing bribes. The Urkupiña Fair they would establish was the product of a group of individuals struggling to find a working alternative to un(der)employment and a way to self-generate income for themselves and their families (Pogliaghi 2008:107).[8] The beginnings of what became La Salada emerged within an economic context, as detailed above, of a neoliberal transformation marked by deproletarianization and informalization.

Yet the founders of the Urkupiña Fair were not the only ones touched by neoliberal restructuring; nor would they be the only entrepreneurs seeing in it possible relief from the shrinking formal economy. In 1994, Argentine and Korean vendors formed Ocean, the second La Salada market (Hacher 2011:40). In 1999, the third fair, Punta Mogote, was established. The foundation of Punta Mogote marked a watershed in the development of La Salada. Jorge Castillo, the administrator of Punta Mogote, did more than anyone to make La Salada a market comprised of state-like organizations by successfully consolidating the means of violence, controlling the extraction of informal taxes, and instigating various structural improvements. Yet before these pseudo state administrations could develop, the logic of the fair was entrenched in violence and threats of force.

FOUNDATIONAL VIOLENCE
IN THE MAKING OF A MARKET

Before becoming the household name in Argentina that it is today, throughout the 1990s La Salada was a "dirty and dilapidated market in an unsafe area," a "liberated territory"—the type where anything goes (Girón 2011:31, 254). As one fair vendor shares, "you had to have balls to go to La Salada at that time" (ibid. 63). In what follows, we inspect the prevalence of violence at the founding of the market, and its place as a central mechanism in establishing access to vital market resources like clients, vendors, and territory. During the 1990s, the risks of violence were multiple. Intramarket conflicts emerged as vendors combatted the consolidation of force and tax extraction by the vendors-turned-managers. And as Urkupiña, then Ocean, and finally Punta Mogote established themselves in the area, turf wars between the three incipient ferias were common.

The violence and "wars"—as Girón (2011) calls them—of La Salada often emerged with fights between the distinct fairs as they jockeyed to establish themselves, gain clientele and workers, and claim their territory. Each addition of a new market challenged the established order; each time, however, the logic remained the same—first make a show of force and negotiate after (Hacher 2011:219). The first of such wars emerged with the foundation of Ocean in 1994, which challenged Urkupiña's exclusive rights. Girón documents the centrality of violence as the ruling logic of interaction and managing competition: "Not the contacts with the municipality, not the arrangements with the police, not the division of the working days. Nothing could stop the growing roughness between Ocean and Urkupiña that saw in their neighbors a lethal competition that was taking their vendors and clients" (2011:85–86). One former Ocean vendor explains his reason for leaving:

the escalation and omnipresent threat of physical violence in response to new competition. "Physical confrontations started to be common," he says, because Urkupiña "wanted to make us disappear . . . the thing became *heavy*" (ibid. 86–87; emphasis in original). Eva, an informal tax collector in Ocean, shares a similar story of violence targeted against the vendors of a competing fair: "I was at the entrance to the pool and I saw various Bolivians beating up a Korean guy. They wanted to take the merchandise that he had to sell . . . Afterward I found out that they were the thugs of Rojas Paz [the administrator of Urkupiña]" (Hacher 2011:38). Similar escalations of violence and a dangerous atmosphere emerged with the founding of Punta Mogote (Girón 2011:90).

Inside the ferias violence was also frequent. Wars were waged between administration and vendors as the former worked to establish itself and to monopolize violence in that territory. According to Charles Bronson (a revealing pseudonym used by the head of security at Punta Mogote),[9] a war started when a group of vendors—who held 30 percent of the Punta Mogote fair—stopped paying taxes. He recounts the violence that ensued: "It was hell. Ten of them would get together and they would throw a stand at your head. They came at us with clubs, with pavers. Afterwards they would go to the courts of Lomas de Zamora and say that here we coerced them, that we were violent. If I show you the photos you won't be able to believe it: this was a war" (Hacher 2011:61). An Urkupiña constituent until 1998 shares, "It was very dangerous . . . every day someone got killed" (Girón 2011:64). Regardless of its inaccuracy, this hyperbolic statement speaks to the phenomenology of grave, violent insecurity in La Salada at that time. Violence was thus present in multiple actor interactions at the feria's founding and yet also the mechanism through which the feria became established and, as we shall see, pacified.

CIVILIZING THE FERIA

In the words of Punta Mogote administrator Jorge Castillo, "Before, this was hell. [Now] not even close" (Girón 2011:232). Today there are very few chances of anyone being assaulted in the passageways of La Salada's markets (ibid. 230). To the extent that violence slowly but progressively vanished from the feria, we can describe it, borrowing from Elias, as a civilizing process.[10] In what follows, we empirically demonstrate how managers and enforcers came to pacify their markets through the dual and symbiotic processes of (1) the establishment of a *monopoly of force*, whereby the means of violence became consolidated under the ferias' administrative apparatuses and (2) *tax extraction*, through which the accumulation of tribute both provided for and necessitated the growth and solidification of those administrations (including their security forces). Through these two intertwined developments (which unfolded with the complicity of law-enforcement agents), violence became expurgated from the social and commercial life of La Salada.

In the beginning, local leaders in La Salada faced the challenge of asserting their leadership in an environment in which all players were more or less equal and all claims to dominance open to contestation. So how did managers and enforcers succeed in concentrating the means of coercion inside the feria and pacifying its operations? Vadim Volkov's (2002) analysis of the fate of the Russian economy in the decade that followed the collapse of socialism provides important insights on this issue. The strife among "violent entrepreneurs," extremely bloody at first, eventually subsided toward the second half of the 1990s. Volkov teases out two mechanisms that account for this trend: selection and collusion. Selection refers to the elimination of weaker entrepreneurs through violence. Sebastián Hacher (2011) describes one such example in La Salada. After the police arrest Castillo and Bronson, both accused of serious injuries against dissenting vendors, Bronson narrates: "They had us like a week in the police station . . . We were beat to shit . . . After going free, Castillo started an offensive against his enemies and he displaced them one by one" (2011:61). Collusion, on the other hand, refers to the emergence of pacts among violent groups, by which each comes to respect the holdings and market shares controlled by others. Girón relays the empirical reality of Volkov's collusion in the pacification of La Salada; Punta Mogote, he writes, reached its truce with Urkupiña after a confrontation where "Castillo demonstrated by force that the best was to try to coexist. If not, tragedy would occur" (2011:146). From that conflict, the ferias reached an agreement whereby a tentative peace began that further solidified over time.

Those managers and enforcers who emerged victorious from the processes of selection and collusion were true "violent specialists," in Tilly's (2003) sense of the term.[11] Yet the violent specialists of La Salada—as many others before and after them (Tilly 2003; Blok 2001; Kakar 1996)—came to deploy not only acts but also threats of violence that sufficiently deterred escalations to violent resolution. Demonstrations of toughness and ruthlessness over time solidified the violent specialists' (and their managers') reputations. Charles Bronson, for example, in the words of Hacher, became "a kind of murderer at rest, that only acted when he had no other choice," because he was now able to "resolve conflicts with a look and two yells" (2011:109). Hacher documents a similar transition with Maguila, an enforcer and tax collector in La Salada: "He doesn't give a shit (*no le importa nada*). If he has to kill you, he kills you . . . [he] seems to have made that custom [into] a profession . . . After I'll find out that it's been a long time that no one is his victim, but that his fame grew independently and works for itself.

Maguila doesn't need to fight anymore. He goes around calmly . . .
It's enough to see him arrive that conflicts are appeased, disputes are settled, debtors pay" (ibid. 65–66).

But it was not only the enforcers who were seen as unchal-
lengeable. More broadly, this became structurally ingrained in
the logic of the fair, as the sole right of the administrations to
wield force was no longer questioned or disputed in any organized way. With time the administrations needed to act out
violent responses to establish their authority with less and less
frequency, as the mere show and knowledge of the existence of
that force was enough to maintain the territories pacified.

One of the main ways the fair administrations achieved this
accepted monopoly, and the consequential pacification of their
territories, was through the amassing and consolidation of the
security arms of their organizations. As with Tilly's (1992) European lords, the resources extracted from the populations under
their command were invested into increasing their military capacities. In La Salada, all the markets have "a group of private
security employees, with uniforms and walkie-talkies" (Pogliaghi 2008:64). In Punta Mogote, for example, administrator
Castillo employs multiple security forces to monitor the inner
workings of his feria, as well as its entry points and perimeter
(Girón 2011:218). Interestingly, many of these "private" security guards once served as part of the state's punitive arm;
Charles Bronson, for example, is a retired sergeant from the
Federal Police (Hacher 2011:17, 48). Each of the three established ferias also maintains a contingent standing army, built
in part from their relationships with clubs of soccer hooligans
(*barra bravas*); each "has personnel that works off the books
prepared for battle. They charge up to $500 per head for a
night of 'services'" (Girón 2011:242).

With the solidification of violent specialists' reputations,
both the administrations and their territory become untouch-
able. A process akin to the one described by Tilly (1992) en-

sued: as lords accumulate their means of force and violently compete over valuable resources—including territory—they cause the formation of pacified territories with increasingly defined boundaries. As Girón (2011:29–30) recounts the story of a shootout between a security official and a nineteen-year-old drug-addicted thief, he underscores the existence of these delineated territories of pacification in La Salada. That youth had made the mistake of attempting to rob in a zone that was pacified, where violent opportunistic crime was not tolerated. Girón contextualizes the confrontation: "It had been months since there was a shootout in La Salada. By the force of years of forced arrangements and delimitations impossible to mark on a map, each shoplifter, petty thief, or drug dealer knows that 'you don't fuck' with certain places (*en ciertos lugares 'no se jode'*)" (ibid. 30).

Tax extraction is also an integral force behind the emergence of the monopoly of violence and consequent territorial pacification. Again, Tilly (1992) helps clarify this by showing that war-making parties need to maximize resource extraction from the populations under their domain in order to fund and increase their capacities for violence. Protection from other lords and from themselves, as Tilly asserts, provides the rationale by which extraction is justified. This symbiotic relationship between tax extraction and the consolidation of force clearly develops over the course of the market's consolidation. Administrators need to collect taxes to cover organizational expenses, including security, while they need those security enforcers to collect the taxes. As Hacher writes, "in La Salada, the informal tax amount equals the firepower the collector demonstrates" (2011:69). In 1999, the administrator Rojas Paz of Urkupiña contracts two former Ocean enforcers—one of them, the infamous enforcer Maguila, who was introduced earlier—to get his vendors to pay their taxes. Before their arrival, Hacher writes, Urkupiña "had cash problems. Of the 500 members, very few paid the 15 pesos for the weekly fee that included the cleaning, security and the bribe the police charged to let them work" (ibid. 67). Maguila's attitude toward this work was undeniably violent; recounting his words from his first day at Urkupiña, "If you have to cut someone's throat, we don't have a problem [doing that]"; in less than a month, those who failed to pay were hardly forty vendors (ibid. 68). Violence secures the extraction of taxes necessary for the functioning of the administration. Yet as the extraction process further develops, so does the administration that manages it.

As Tilly (1992) shows with the European mercantilists, with the institutionalization of collecting increasing dues in the feria, a bureaucracy grows that further consolidates power within the hands of the managers and their administrative organizations. Early on, the Urkupiña vendors voted in assembly to have two individuals serve as administrators; they became responsible for distributing the stalls, collecting money, and sorting out arrangements with the police (Girón 2011:53). Yet as these administrators accrued power in their fairs—through a particularly successful recipe of deceipt, astute leadership, and coercion—the dues extracted grew as they came to cover a wide range of services and infrastructural investments. Pogliaghi recounts the increasing expansion of the state-like organizations' involvements with its territories as follows:

> They (i) ensure compliance with local regulations (such as providing parking, drinking water, bathrooms, sweeping and cleaning, waste collection, hire an emergency medical service, guarantee the services of light, electricity and security inside and the surroundings of the venue); (ii) charge stallholders a fee to cover the costs of running the show; (iii) manage—in some cases—the renting of stalls; (iv) arrange with the administrators of the other ferias the hours of operation (although the municipal ex-

ecutive power is the one legally authorized to set the days and times); and (v) act as the withholding agent of the Health, Safety and Hygiene Tax, a fee charged to the activities on the premises and that is payable to the Municipality. (2008:55)[12]

Beyond the state-like services provided, these administrations also developed the feria's infrastructure. Originally, La Salada was a space where, as one former vendor recounts, when it rained, it flooded horribly: "there was a terrible smell of urine," and "people would eat and throw their trash on the ground, which joined with a permanent layer of pig fat that invaded everything" (Girón 2011:63). Administrators began to designate taxes to address that, in the words of one vendor, La Salada was a "pigsty" (ibid. 64). Administrators used the monthly expenses and extra taxes to fill the swimming pools (which had remained unaddressed and only accumulated trash); provide roofing, food courts, and parking lots; put in drains and sewers; asphalt the surrounding streets; cut trees; and contract private security (ibid. 108–9 and 124–25). Through these strategic investments in infrastructure, intertwined with the processes of tax extraction and violence consolidation outlined above, the administrators came to secure (in more ways than one) the operations of the feria.

In contrast to Tilly's European warlords, however, the emergence of feria administrations with coercive and extractive capacities occurred within the territory of an already existing state. Far from sitting by idly as the market developed and violence raged (or, later, subsided), the state and its agents intervened in a variety of forms, for a variety of reasons, playing a crucial role in the market's development and the incidence of violence within it. Disorganized interventions by police officials seeking illicit financial gains through coercion and bribes was one of the original impetus for La Salada's tax-extracting organizations. The administration of Urkupiña, for example, emerged to barter arrangements with the police and municipality (Girón 2011). In other words, a major factor behind the rise and establishment of managers was their ability to organize and centralize bribe collection and channel money (the very stuff of the arrangements, or *arreglos*) to state officials (ibid. 52, 54).

It is also important to note that during the period of foundational violence, the punitive arm of the state played a structuring role through judicial and police interventions, and served as another resource mobilized by feria administrators in wars of market competition. There was, for example, frequent recourse to the state judicial system when stallholders believed the administrators were getting out of hand (Girón 2011). However, the effectiveness of this judicial action was dubious; Castillo, for example, boasts that he has the highest number of lawsuits against him in the country. More decisively, the punitive arm of the state, especially its provincial police force, intervened when activated (and paid for) by powerful stakeholders inside the market. The managers of Urkupiña, for example, took advantage of their close relationships with some agents in the local municipal government and state police to make life difficult for Punta Mogote (ibid. 143). A case in point is the police arrest of Castillo and Charles Bronson, both accused of serious injuries against the opposing *feriantes*. While these relationships with the state's punitive arm were never the exclusive factor in the resolution of the "wars of competition" between the ferias, they played a crucial role in shaping La Salada's development, and also demonstrate the state's complicity in both the market's foundational violence and its pacification.

These days, rather than intervening punitively against informal market participants, the state works to protect and regulate its operation. When the market is open, the gendarmerie patrols the neighborhood, and "police controls . . . were indi-cated by all the *feriantes* interviewed" (Pogliaghi 2008:49). Bribe extraction, furthermore, became institutionalized to the point of constituting an intricate shadow tax system (Dewey 2014). Dewey estimates that the total amount collected monthly in La Salada by state agents equals more than $770,000 (ibid. 12) These informal taxes are significant sums "upon which the state budget" and "the performance of local and provincial governments" now depend (ibid. 15).

In summary, once the fair administrations had shown their force to their competitors, their own vendors, and the neighborhood, and through these conflicts established their monopoly on violence, they did what made the most economic sense for them all: in the words of Castillo, to show "Argentina that you could come without problems" (Girón 2011:212). As such, driven by a moneymaking logic, the most successful violent specialists made the market more lucrative by instigating the pacification of those same territories, and by dedicating funds to develop its infrastructure, including its security apparatus. The unintended outcome of increased business, however, is that violence (often linked with opportunistic crime)—expunged from the feria—migrates to its immediate adjacencies. Girón introduces this spatial relationship of internal pacification and external depacification:

> The existence of "liberated points" for delinquency, the marketing of drugs and other illicit [items] is mainly thanks to the complicity of certain police agents in the area . . . [But] also, by the silence of those responsible for the big ferias, [only] worried in a selfish fashion that nothing strange happens within the limits of their small piece of land. "My land has its border; as long as that border is respected, *outside they can do what they want*," . . . explains Jorge Castillo. (ibid. 232; our emphasis)

VIOLENCE OUTSIDE THE STREET MARKET: DECIVILIZING

Crime data, interviews with primary informants (physicians and law enforcement agents), and ethnographic fieldwork point to two basic facts: daily life in the neighborhood became more violent during the last two decades, and violent episodes increase during the days when La Salada opens to the public (typically twice a week). These days violent crime has reached unprecedented levels. As stated above, homicides in Arquitecto Tucci increased 180 percent since 2007. The murder rate is four times that of the state of Buenos Aires. Home to roughly 28 percent of the total population of the district of Lomas de Zamora, Arquitecto Tucci had 58 percent of its homicides in 2012 (CSJN 2013).

As described in the introduction, physicians who work in the emergency rooms at the local hospital and local urgent care unit (UPA) confirm the skyrocketing of interpersonal violence, and they all agree that the important variations within this high frequency are related to the operation of the street market. The two days a week in which the street fair is open, there is a noticeable increase in the number of injuries. One ER doctor highlights the correlation between violence and market operation, and implicitly puts forward an explanation that revolves around what criminologists call "opportunistic crime": "The street fair is a source of conflict. There's an increase in interpersonal aggression during the days its markets open to the public. Thousands of people come with cash to buy [goods] or with merchandise to sell. There are many robberies, lots of them at gunpoint."

Law enforcement agents have a similar understanding. "When the market is closed," says the local police chief, "Tucci is a normal neighborhood." But La Salada, he continues, "adds a special seasoning" to the neighborhood because "it brings more than 50,000 people every time it opens its doors . . . a number of people that equals the number that attends a big soccer match."

On the basis of newspaper accounts, we mapped twenty-seven homicides between 2009 and 2013. Sixteen of them occurred in an area less than half a mile from the feria, most of them after a robbery attempt (half occurred less than two blocks from the feria). Robberies at gunpoint are indeed very frequent around the market, and they sometimes end badly. In May 2012, a twenty-two-year-old resident was killed after being attacked by a group of four, and a trader was shot in the back and murdered after a robbery attempt in July of that same year.

During 2010, the local media reported seven murders. Among these episodes, there were crimes committed during robberies of La Salada merchants or shoppers and others that had the appearance of being "retributions," which in the local parlance is known as "settling debts" (*ajuste de cuentas*). In 2011, a twenty-three-year-old man was lynched by a group of neighbors when he tried to rob a house—he died from the punches and stoning.[13] In that same month, another young man, twenty-one years old, was found murdered with two shots in his throat and in his back, and a thirty-year-old man who had been stabbed by two attackers while driving his truck died while he was being attended to at the local hospital.[14] Months later, a federal police officer was murdered by two people who stole his car. The sergeant received a fatal gunshot wound to the chest.[15] The crime reports of 2012 began with the death of a two-year-old boy who died after being shot in the back by a man who was trying to stop three robbers from assaulting his wife and brother-in-law.[16] In May, a young twenty-two-year-old man died after being shot at by four people near La Salada.[17] In July, a stallholder was murdered by a shot in the back after a robbery attempt, and another person died in a shootout with the police after raiding a number

32 bus.[18] The month of October was particularly violent. An eighteen-year-old young man was injured by a bullet and died while being attended to at the local hospital; another man was murdered with two shots while resisting an alleged attempted robbery in his house; the owner of a sewing workshop in the neighborhood was shot in the chest and died while being attended to at Redael Hospital; and a little girl was injured after receiving a bullet to her throat.[19]

Our ethnographic material corroborates the trends highlighted by these violent crime rates and key informants. The huge and varied amount of merchandise and the millions of pesos that traverse in and out of the market through the streets of this poor and relegated neighborhood present innumerable opportunities for crime—mainly for the poor youth who "crushed by the weight of chronic unemployment and underemployment . . . continue to look to the 'booty capitalism' of the streets (as Max Weber would say) for the means to survive, to obtain desirable consumer goods, and to realize the values of the masculine ethos of honor, if not to escape from the grind of day-to-day destitution" (Wacquant 2008:60). "During the days the market is open," thirty-seven-year-old Verónica tells us, "we lock ourselves inside the house. Those days, there are a lot of robberies and there's always a crazy kid with a gun, and they start shooting at each other, and one of my children can get hurt." And on numerous occasions, such as the story of Lucho, which opens this book, residents described to us murders or other violent episodes that took place near La Salada.

Eleven-year-old Roberto tells us: "My dad was at the fair yesterday and there were some guys who wanted to rob a van and he thought they were going to rob him. He grabbed one and tried to cover himself with one arm. The other guy hit him with an iron bar and broke it [his dad's arm]." Then he adds that his ten-year-old friend has a gun that "he uses to rob at the feria, with his brother, who is older. They steal clothes and then he distributes it among his friends, who are also thieves, and they sell it." Forty-year-old Graciela agrees: "kids in the neighborhood know that people from very different places come to the feria, and they take advantage of this, and they rob there. You see them every time there is a feria; they go there and they come back with bags full of things, stolen things. And they have their pockets full of [stolen] cash. They show the money to us, and they offer stolen goods for sale." After warning us that "here you have to be careful," forty-six-year-old Mariela tells us about the murder of sixteen-year-old Carlitos, who was "trying to rob a van that was coming out of the market when the driver shot him."

With the development of the street market, the area adjacent to it thus became what environmental criminologists call a "cluster of criminal opportunities" or a "high activity node" (Bratingham and Bratingham 1993:11). Aware of the increasing violence, feria managers have recently begun to secure the surrounding area with their own private security guards. Twice a week, well-armed uniformed men and women with bullet-proof vests (some of them off-duty cops from the neighborhood) form what are locally known as "safety corridors" (*corredores de seguridad*) in some streets of the neighborhood through which clients and merchants move in and out of the market.

Opportunities for local youth to engage in petty crime are not simply objective ones (merchandise and cash) but also subjective—many of our interviewees, as we will see in further detail in chapter 4, perceive that the area is understood as a "no-man's-land." In the course of formal interviews and informal conversations, residents express their feeling that the neighborhood, and not surprisingly the area around the feria, is a "liberated zone": an area where perpetrators of all sorts of illicit activities can do as they please (or, as one neighbor put it at a community meeting devoted to discussing issues of safety and crime, a place where "anything goes").

La Salada is not the only source of violence. Small "bands" (e.g., La Banda del Gordo Mario, La Banda de los Guille, and Los Corsarios) devoted to the storage, preparation, and distribution of drugs are reported to have operated in Arquitecto Tucci and its surrounding area, fueling part of this rise in interpersonal violence (Sain 2009). During our fieldwork, many police operations, some of them including exchanges of gunshots between police agents and dealers, seized dozens of kilograms of cocaine and thousands of doses of freebase cocaine (FBC), locally known as *paco*.[20]

Both local residents and people who do not live but only work in the area as teachers, social workers, or doctors agree in that, in terms of public violence (the violence witnessed or experienced on the streets), Tucci is indeed a more dangerous place than in the past. Having known the area for more than two decades, we can confidently say that this is indeed the case—that it is not just a media-fed "feeling" or a "sense" of insecurity. Locals get injured and killed at higher rates than before and, as a consequence, residents are more fearful of others and of their surroundings. The opposite is true for what happens within the physical confines of La Salada—the interpersonal violence that affected shoppers and traders in the past has indeed decreased. Daily life in Tucci is now more unpredictable and more insecure. In Elias's terms, the social world of Tucci residents has been *depacified*. While La Salada has been "civilized," the neighborhood is experiencing a *decivilizing process*. Everyday life becomes more subjected to "sudden reversals of fortune," and violence becomes an oftentimes "unavoidable and everyday event" (Elias 1994:450, 448).

This chapter has described the interlinked dynamics behind this process of civilization and depacification. The next three chapters will provide further empirical details about the kinds of (public and private) violence in the area while expanding the scope of analysis to include other uses and forms of interpersonal physical aggression, inspect its relationship with the intermittent, contradictory, and selective state action(s), and explore its political and ethical dimensions. As we move forward in the analysis, the reader will be able to see how depacification and concatenations of violence are interwoven in real time and space.

CHAPTER 2

BORN AMID BULLETS
CONCATENATED VIOLENCE(S)

Seated at the base of the flagpole, recess has hardly begun. Samanta and Pedro, two of my fourth graders, chat lively. Pedro asks: "And your dad, does he have a bullet scar? [*¿se le hizo cascarita el tiro?*]." Samanta responds: "No . . . My dad's shots are old."

Fernanda's field notes, April 2012

Monday, April 23, 2012. Today Darío died. He was seventeen years old. Nobody knows if he killed himself or if he was killed. He entered the school where Fernanda teaches. The teachers weren't there because there was a strike of assistant personnel and they weren't giving classes. Darío was disoriented; it's believed he was under the influence of drugs. In the school they tried to restrain him. They called the hospital so they would send an ambulance or a doctor. No one came. Half an hour later, with clear signs of paranoia, according to those who saw him, Darío ran out of the school. He carried a slingshot in his hand with which he threatened the ghosts that he said he saw. After an hour, the principal received news that Darío had died. He had drowned in the swampy, rotten creek that crosses the adjoining settlement to the school. They say in the neighborhood that he had a fight with some neighbors and ended up in the river, bogged down, and that he couldn't get out. They had the wake at his house. His death wasn't reported in any newspaper. Days before, the neighbors say that Darío had been violently attacked by the local police. "They mistook him for a thief [*chorrito*]; they got him in the police car and they beat the shit out of him [*lo cagaron a palos*]," they tell us with fear of possible reprisals. "If they see him drugged, why don't they take him home?" They also say that when Darío left the school, he attacked some neighbors. They didn't call the police (why would they if, as they have recounted to us many times, "the cops always arrive late"?), but took justice into their own hands and punished Darío. Nobody knows and maybe no one wants to know if they were the ones that threw him in the contaminated and lethal creek.

During two and a half years of fieldwork, Fernanda worked with three different groups of students (third, fourth, and sixth graders ages eight to thirteen) in Arquitecto Tucci. Among these students, shootings, armed robberies, and street fights are habitual topics of conversation, regularly present in their daily lives. In other words, violence does not need to be "brought up" by the ethnographer as a "theme" to be discussed and analyzed. During our fieldwork, not a week went by without one or more of the sixty elementary schoolchildren describing one or more episodes involving one or more forms of violence. Between June 2009 and June 2012, Fernanda's students brought up twenty-two cases of violent death. These included the deaths of former classmates, such as Lucho; of residents, such as Darío; and of family members or acquaintances near La Salada.

More or less trivial occasions inside the classroom—the

mentioning of a relative's birthday or a history lesson—became opportunities to talk about the latest violent episode in the neighborhood. In what follows we present a series of field notes (written by Fernanda) that capture the public and frequent character of violence in the area. For her students, violence is all but extraordinary.

> May 5, 2010. "In May 1810," Fernanda reads aloud from the social science textbook to the fourth graders, "the King of Spain was deposed by Napoleon Bonaparte. Jailed in France . . ." "Teacher, teacher . . ." Carlos (age nine) interrupts, "my uncle is also in jail . . . I think he is in for robbery." Another student, Matu (also age nine), then adds: "Right around my house, there's one guy who is a thief, but never went to jail . . . he has a new car." Suddenly, the lesson on the May Revolution becomes a collective report on the latest events in the neighborhood:
>
> JOHNY (*ten*): Do you know that Savalita was killed? Seven shots . . . some dealers wanted to steal his motorcycle.
>
> TATIANA (*nine*): No, it wasn't like that. Savalita was the one who wanted the motorcycle. He tried to steal it from a drug dealer. Word, I knew him!
>
> JOHNY: No, it was his motorcycle.
>
> MARIO (*nine*): My neighbor is a drug dealer. The cops come and never do anything.
>
> TATIANA: Cops like to use drugs!
>
> Tuesday, September 6, 2011. "Miss, yesterday my mom turned fifty," says Romina, visibly happy, loud enough so that everyone in the classroom could hear. "My uncle had his birthday last week!" Paula says and then, without chang-

ing her tone or expression, she adds, "But the other day he died. He was drunk and fighting with his wife. She hit him, threw the barbeque in his face and when she went to lift him up he was dead." Paula's story acted as the trigger for the following dialogue:

TAMARA: My uncle, miss, yesterday he got into a gunfight [*se agarraron a los tiros*] and he almost got killed [*casi le dan*]. He had to leave running.

ROMINA: And my stepdad . . . he was drunk from drinking with the guys, and some people wanted to steal his sneakers and he said to them, "I know you," and so they shot him in the leg.

TAMARA: And the other day . . . my little brother and I were at the door and there were two guys on a motorcycle that the police were following and they stopped close to my house and the police surrounded them all and shot twice in the air and my little brother almost had an attack; we ran away.

Monday, April 11, 2011. Fernanda enters the classroom a few seconds later than her students. She sees a small metal beam sticking out of the window overlooking the courtyard. She gets on the chair and, seeing that it was practically loose (part of the interior window frame was rusted and about to fall), she pulls it out and puts it on top of the cabinet. Roberto, one of her students asks her, "What is that, miss?"

FERNANDA: A piece of metal [*un fierro*]; I don't know what it's doing here. It's dangerous; I'm going to hold on to it.

She hears whispering and laughter among them, until Lautaro, from the back of the classroom, shouts at Roberto.

LAUTARO: Man, Roberto, it's like your friend's iron piece [*fierro*]!

Roberto explains to Fernanda that a friend of his has an "iron piece," but "of the other kind."

FERNANDA: A friend of yours has a gun? How old is he?

ROBERTO: He's ten years old. He robs in the feria, with his brother who is older.

FERNANDA: How is a little ten-year-old boy going to steal?

CHELITA: Sure . . . he lives in el Bajo. There they're all thieves [*chorros*]. He steals clothes there at the feria, and he shares it between his friends who are thieves like him, and they sell it.

Thursday, September 1, 2011. "The values that our founding father José de San Martín defended are values that are still very important today. Respect, Justice . . . and you all can use this in your everyday life: don't mess with your class-mates [*no cargarse entre compañeros*], respect yourself, don't insult your mothers, respect them." Like this Fernanda begins another of her lessons, this time on the legacy of "The Liberator of America," when Ariela, her student, inter-rupted her: "Miss, miss, you know Luisito, right?" Fernanda remembered Luis fondly. He was one of those curious boys, a little mischievous. "Yes, of course, he was a student of mine two years ago." "They call him *fierrito* now," says Ariela, "be-cause he always goes about with *un fierro* [a gun] at his waist and he tells people: 'Look what I have.'" The world of *fierrito* (little gun) is not foreign to Ariela. Her father just got out of jail after serving a sentence for robbery. Her brother is a fugitive, accused of knifing his friend to death (*asesinar a puñaladas a un amigo*).

Those children and adolescents who hear a story about a relative behind bars (or have a relative doing time) are the same ones who speak about the scars left by bullets, the same ones who touch one another's wounds, that listen to a story about (or witness) the death of an adolescent on the day of his birthday, or who describe how a relative (or less frequently, stranger) tried to rape a girl, or how an uncle beat an aunt. For them, shootings, injuries, and death (and jail time) have an ordinary character ("my dad has a gun because sometimes people want to grab a piece of the land we occupied in the squatter settlement and we shoot at them [*los cagamos a tiros*]. Here, things are done that way—*a los tiros*." "Every night there are shootings, people are selling drugs and the dealers shoot at each other"). For the children and adolescents living in Tucci, their daily life experiences—as seen through the cognitive relationships they establish with past events, such as the May Revolution or the life of San Martín, and through the types of threats they launch at each other ("I'm going to put a bullet in your head")—are permeated with both interpersonal and state violence. For children and adolescents—and as we will describe shortly, adults too—violence pervades everyday life.

Among psychiatrists, much debate has revolved around "desensitization" to community violence (McCart et al. 2007; Guerra, Huesman, and Spindler 2003). If by desensitization or habituation we mean simply familiarization—as when the children say, time and again, "we are used to it"—then we think that based on what they say, and the way in which they say it, we could argue, paraphrasing Foucault, that violence for them is in the "order of barrio things." If by habituation or desensitization, however, we mean that children are less likely to notice or pay attention to incidents of violence, then the above stories and dozens of pages of Fernanda's notes, in which children talk almost compulsively about the latest shootout or murder, should prove that they are far from habituated. The drawings in figures 17–21, made as part of an exercise in which students were asked to describe the positive and negative aspects of their neighborhood, provide further evidence of this. In the first drawing, a third grade student portrays his barrio through *se tiran tiro* (they shoot at each other) and the lone presence of a police car. A year later, two fourth graders and a

FIGURE 17. Shooting at each other.

FIGURE 18. "The things I like; the things I don't like."

FIGURE 19. Likes and dislikes.

FIGURE 20. Drugs, garbage, robberies, and rats.

FIGURE 21. Shootings.

sixth grader depict their neighborhood along similar lines. The drawings encapsulate a shared viewpoint among Fernanda's students: most of them like "playing soccer" and dislike the gunshots, fights, and killings.

Elementary schoolchildren see themselves as growing up in the crossfire, a sentiment shared by the anonymous artist of the following graffiti outside their school: "I was born amid bullets, I was raised among thieves" (*Entre balas he nacido, entre chorros me he criado*) (figure 22). A few blocks from the school where Fernanda works, two murals provide a visual reminder of the lethal consequences of this violence (figures 23 and 24). Sixteen-year-old Acho was killed four years ago when a local storeowner shot him, presumably during an attempted robbery. Dani, nineteen, was murdered three years ago under similar circumstances.

March 30, 2010: Marita asks me if I know Naria's father. I tell her that I don't. "He is in heaven; he was shot in the head."

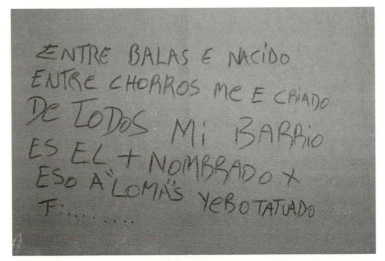

FIGURE 22. "I was born amid bullets, I was raised among thieves."

FIGURE 23. Mural remembering the dead.

April 8, 2010: Samantha tells me that her neighbor, Carlitos, was turning seventeen this past Sunday: "A friend of his came to pick him up to go around the neighborhood. Carlitos didn't want to go, because it was his birthday. But his friend

FIGURE 24. Mural remembering the dead.

persuaded him and off they went." Samantha tells me that she thinks they were armed. Carlitos was killed. "Once dead, his friends carried him around the block [as in a procession]. I went to the funeral. His eyes were still open, and his house [where the funeral was taking place] was full of his friends. Carlitos had many friends. The bullet came into his chest and made a tiny little hole there. But the bullet went out through his back. The hole there was huge."

October 3, 2011: Luis tells me that yesterday two neighbors got into a fight and shot at each other. One "shot the other in the leg . . . the bullet went through his knee. First they screamed at each other, then they punched each other, and then they began shooting [*se cagaron a tiros*]."

Children and adolescents growing up in this neighborhood not only encounter criminal and police violence, but domestic and sexual violence frequently put their lives in danger as well, either as victims or as witnesses.

October 17, 2011: Brian tells me that yesterday he got mad at his uncle. "He beat my aunt; he always beats her."

October 20, 2011: Miriam looks at my cell phone and tells me: "My mom had the same phone, but my father broke it. He already broke two of hers . . . when he gets drunk, he breaks her stuff, and sometimes he beats her too."

October 13, 2009: Julio's mother called the school today. She wanted to talk to her son. During the break, I spoke with Julio. He told me that his mom had to leave their house over the weekend because "my dad had been drinking and he beat the shit out of her. My dad is a slacker; he doesn't have a job. My mom gives him money and he spends it on wine. On Saturday, my mom asked him to turn the volume of the music down and he slapped her in the face, and then he grabbed her hair and dragged her through the house. He also destroyed all the things in the house."

October 15, 2009: Julio's mother came to the school today. She confirmed to me what happened a few days ago. She asked me to observe Julio to make sure he has not been beaten by his dad. In my presence, she also asked her son, Julio, to take good care of his sister because she is afraid her dad will sexually abuse her [Julio's sister].

March 19, 2012: To commemorate International Women's Day, Fernanda proposed a collective exercise for her sixth graders: that they would make a "tree of wishes." The assignment was very simple: "Write down on paper what you want for women on their day." Besides the typical clichés ("peace," "love"), José, one of the most sharp and inquisitive students, wrote: "No to rape, no to oral(s) [*No a las violaciones ni a los orales*; reference to forced oral sex]." The colorful sheet with the "Tree of Wishes" today adorns one of the peeling walls of Fernanda's classroom.

One risk is more likely to affect girls than boys in these neigh-borhoods: sexual violence. Referring to the presence of *violines* (those who *violan*, i.e., rapists) and suggesting one of the ways in which different kinds of violence relate to one another, Noelia (nine) tells Fernanda that "my cousin was almost raped yester-day [a few blocks from the school]. Neighbors went to the home of those *violines* and kicked their door down." "What are the *violines?*" Fernanda innocently asks the class. "Those who make you [have] babies," eight-year-old Josiana answers matter-of-factly. This, as we will see, was not an isolated episode.

FROM RETALIATION TO CONCATENATION

Both the persistence and increase of interpersonal violence in urban settings have been associated with a number of fac-tors, from economic status, ethnic heterogeneity, and residen-tial mobility in now classic studies (Shaw and McKay 1942; Kornhauser 1978) to the prevalence and interdependence of both informal and formal community networks (Sampson and Groves 1989; Sampson 2012) and more political variables, such as electoral competition and factionalization (Villareal 2002). While the social-scientific study of aggregate charac-teristics correlated with crime and violence has produced some superb refinements and extensions of social control theory (Sampson and Groves 1989; Sampson, Raudenbush, and Earls 1997; Villareal 2002) and highlighted the "risk" and "protec-tive" factors that give rise to or deter violence (Turpin and Kurtz 1997; Muggah 2012), it has deftly sidestepped one key issue first spotlighted by students of "street justice" (Jacobs 2004; Mullins, Wright, and Jacobs 2004; Jacobs and Wright 2006): the uses and forms of interpersonal violence.

According to sociologists Bruce Jacobs and Richard Wright, "[A] substantial number of assaults, robberies, and other forms of serious criminal behavior are a direct consequence of retaliation and counter-retaliation. . . . [R]etaliatory conflicts contribute significantly to the violent reputation and reality of many high-crime neighborhoods" (2006:5; see also Jacobs 2004). Retaliation is "widely threatened and used by urban street criminals to deter and punish predators"(Mullins, Wright, and Jacobs 2004:911). Street criminal violence has, in this approach, one main form—that of a dyadic exchange governed by the norm of reciprocity—and one chief use: that of retaliation. Violence is thus seen as the result of a *lex talionis*, a payback for prior offenses; or, in a recent approach, a Maussian "gift" of sorts, a "gesture that, if accepted, demands to be reciprocated" (Papachristos 2009:80): you assault my friend, so I try to kill you—tit for tat (D. Black 1983; Jacobs and Wright 2006). Much of this interpersonal violence, so these studies tell us, remains confined to dyadic relationships.

Ethnographic and journalistic accounts of violence in both Latin American shantytowns and US high-poverty enclaves, whether ghettos or inner cities (Kotlowitz 1991; Bourgois 1995; Anderson 1999; Alarcón 2003, 2009; LeBlanc 2004; Venkatesh 2008; Jones 2009; Harding 2010), attest to the fact that direct retaliation (i.e., "the retribution for a past dispute by the aggrieved or a member of the aggrieved's group against the person or group responsible for the original affront" [Papachristos 2009:81]) sculpts much of the violence.[1] Many ethnographic and qualitative studies also show that a "search for respect" (Bourgois 1995), not necessarily retaliatory in a strict dyadic sense, is at the foreground of violent practices (Rodgers 2006; Jones 2009; Zubillaga 2009; Penglase 2010).

One episode that unfolded before journalist Cristian Alarcón's eyes, and that is vividly reconstructed in his masterful *Cuando Me Muera Quiero que Me Toquen Cumbia*, encapsulates this retaliatory character of violence. Over the previous six months, sixteen-year-old Brian had robbed many residents, young and old, in a poor neighborhood in Buenos Aires and had threatened to kill a youngster named Rana after Rana had punched one of Brian's closest friends (from the street gang Los Sapitos). One summer afternoon, residents had had enough and were about to take justice into their own hands—ready, according to Alarcón's eyewitness account, to kill him. High on pills and alcohol, gun in hand, Brian was now publicly defying those who were after him:

> Brian . . . short, blond hair, with the chest of a creature of 12, face pulsing like someone possessed from the effects of three days of pills and alcohol . . . over the hot asphalt of General Pinto street, half-naked, dressed only in a pair of soccer shorts; he beat his chest with his left hand and twirled the gun with the ring finger of his right. In front of him, across the width of the asphalt, multiplying, was the mob, insulting him, ready to sacrifice him. Men from every alley, youth and veterans, grabbed weapons buried in their closets and at the bottom of drawers, eager to eliminate him . . . Ten meters away, on General Pinto street, Brian yelled, spit, insulted. Fags! Fags! Snitches! Brian had wanted to kill a kid from the barrio, El Rana. You hit my friend—he said. El Rana had had a falling out with one of the Sapitos. Brian emptied his gun with terrible aim. It didn't take long for the neighbors to appear, each one individually armed. Brian retreated when he saw a dozen armed men coming after him. (2003:129–42)

Retaliation, in the form of "settling debts," was also common in La Salada as exemplified in the murder of Oscar Garín, a noncommissioned officer of the prison service who worked as a private security guard at one of the warehouses (*galpones*). Garín was found dead in early August 2010 with a shot in the head. The week before his passing, he had been fired from the fair, but apparently he would have retained an important quantity of money (some "change" of 20,000 pesos [about $5,000 in

2011], depending on the version) that he had charged after "arbitrating" a territorial dispute in a sector adjacent to the feria. As Sebastián Hacher, author of the illuminating chronicle about the internal dynamics of the feria, describes:

> The dispute erupted last month in front of the warehouse of the May 27 Cooperative, where Garín worked. One of the days of the feria, a group of burly men arrived early and tried to occupy part of the street where for years a cooperative has worked. When the other stallholders rebuked them, the new occupants tried to justify themselves: "We bought a meter and a half (5 feet) of street: we gave 20,000 pesos to Ramón," they said. Ramón was one of the nicknames of penitentiary worker Oscar Garín, who some also called "El Negro." The week before in the feria there was a kind of confrontation between Garín and those who claimed to be buyers of the place. The prison guard denied having participated in the ploy. That day they threatened him again. They told him: "You cheated us, you're dead." But "El Negro" didn't think much of it. That day he was fired from his job as a guard. A week later they killed him.[2]

Our long-term ethnographic fieldwork, however, reveals that the search for retaliation or respect is not the only purpose of violence. Violence, we will show, is also used to advance or defend territory, discipline children, defend self and property, acquire economic resources, and establish dominance within the household; in other words, violence is deployed to solve many pressing problems. Restricted reciprocity is not the only form that interpersonal violence takes. True, many a violent action that we either witnessed or reconstructed in its immediate aftermath sought to avenge a past verbal or physical attack, either individually (a punch in response to an insult) or collectively (vigilante violence in response to an attempted rape). But once we focus sustained and systematic ethnographic attention on the multiple forms of interpersonal physical aggression that take place both inside homes and outside in the streets, we begin to detect that violence transcends the one-on-one exchange, moving outside the dyadic relationship, and involves other actors who were not part of the original dispute. Instead of reciprocity confined to a delimited sequence, a bounded dispute over dominance (Gould 2003), we uncover a violence that seems to follow the course of diffused reciprocity where the "definition of equivalence is less precise, one's partners may be viewed as a group rather than particular actors, and the sequence of events is less narrowly bounded" (Keohane 1986:4). A more comprehensive understanding of the interpersonal violence that is shaking poor people's daily lives in contemporary Buenos Aires should approach it not solely as a reciprocal exchange confined to a dyadic interaction but also as a set of interconnected events.

Across the social sciences, research on diverse forms of violence remains "specialized and balkanized" (Jackman 2002:387). Students of "family violence" (Tolan et al. 2006; Kurst-Swanger and Petcosky 2003; Gelles 1985), for example, rarely engage in conversations with researchers of street or gang violence (Jones 2009; Harding 2010; Venkatesh 2008; McCart et al. 2007; Bourgois 1995), even when the latter do recurrently detect the mutual influence between private and public forms of brutality; ethnographic and journalistic descriptions attest that violence outside the home usually travels inside and vice versa (see, for example, Bourgois 1995; LeBlanc 2004; Kotlowitz 1991). The study of violence is also highly compartmentalized in psychological studies where there is "very little crossover" in the examination of different types of violence (Tolan et al. 2006:558).

Although analyses of diverse types of violence have remained siloed, a number of scholars have begun to highlight their theoretical and empirical interconnections. Randal Collins, for example, focuses on the theoretical connections between a vast array of seemingly unrelated violent interactions. "[A]ll types of violence," he writes, "fit a small number of patterns for circumventing the barrier of tension and fear that rises up whenever people come into antagonistic confrontation" (2008:8). In other words, for Collins, distinct types of violence share a "situational dynamic" (ibid. 7). Mary Jackman (2002) and Elijah Anderson (1999) have pointed out the shared origins or similar outcomes of a wide variety of private and public, interpersonal and collective, violence. Jackman notes that violence is a "genus of behaviors, made up of a diverse class of injurious actions, involving a variety of behaviors, injuries, motivations, agents, victims, and observers" (2002:404). According to her, "the sole thread connecting [this diversity] is the threat or outcome of injury" (ibid.). Anderson (1999), in turn, underlines the common source shared by many instances of violence. In Anderson's rendition of US inner-city life, the "code of the street" diffuses from the street into homes, schools, parks, and commercial establishments; permeates face-to-face relations; feeds predatory crime and the drug trade; exacerbates interpersonal violence; and even warps practices of courtship, mating, and intimacy (see also Jones 2009). Diverse forms of violence, according to Anderson, can be traced back to the pernicious influence of a bellicose mind-set.

Although inspired by this literature, which underscores empirical commonalities and theoretical analogies, our analysis draws more heavily on a strand of social scientific research that has called attention to the intertwining of different forms of violence. Caroline Moser and Cathy McIlwaine (2004), for example, highlight the causal connections between social, economic, and political violence. Along similar lines, Nancy Scheper-Hughes and Philippe Bourgois (2003) explore linkages between structural, symbolic, everyday, and intimate forms of violence. Calling attention to the "continuum" formed by "peace-time crimes" or "little violences," Bourgois (2009) and Scheper-Hughes (1996; 1997) inspect the typically obscure nexuses between visible forms of violence, "whether criminal, delinquent, or self-inflicted" (Bourgois 2009:18), and less visible ones, "structural, symbolic, and/or normalized" (ibid.). Concentrating on different forms of sexual violence, Liz Kelly (1988) also describes a "continuum." In her case, the notion emphasizes commonalities (i.e., the shared "common character") between the types of violence that buttress patriarchy. Finally, Hume's (2009) and Wilding's (2013) gendered analyses of violence unearth the copresence and overlapping of diverse forms of physical aggression in the everyday life of marginalized communities in postwar El Salvador and contemporary Brazil, respectively. Hume's feminist perspective is of particular importance for the analysis that follows in that it challenges normative understandings of violence as "essentially public and masculinist." As she states, most analyses of violence in Latin America

> are heavily reliant on an exclusively public reading of security. This belies the fact that much of the violence that affects women and children occurs in the home. The result of this separation between "public" security and the safety of women and children has multiple implications. This approach misses historic practices of violence and keeps them hidden from public scrutiny. It also offers an incomplete analysis of violence, ignoring important linkages between violence in the home and violence in the street. (2009:4)

Our examination of the uses and forms of violence in Arquitecto Tucci complements and extends Hume's (and Wilding's) in that it concentrates not only on the copresence of diverse types of physical aggression but on the lateral connections between them—that is, on the many instances in which one form of violence leads to another. In other words, the focus of this chapter lies neither in the ways in which different forms of violence originate from some shared source (or result in a similar outcome) nor in the theoretical associations between them. We are mainly concerned with the uses of (and the horizontal, empirical concatenations between) diverse forms of violence—traditionally studied as separate entities—in the real time and space of a materially and symbolically deprived community. As stated above, focusing on the uses and the interlinking (an empirical exercise that demands detectivelike skills) leads us to consider violence as a repertoire to address individual and collective grievances.

Retaliatory violence abounds in the neighborhood (a dealer misses a payment or consumes part of what he was supposed to sell and then he encounters threats or physical punishment from whoever is above him in the chain of command, a wife resorts to violence against her abusive partner, etc.). But sometimes this dyadic retaliation is part of a larger sequence of events—the dealer who misses a payment hides in his mother's house and, out of frustration or in a desperate attempt to control his addiction, she beats him; he fights with his brother over something he stole to buy drugs; or he invites the fury of his creditor who threatens not only him but his entire family.

As we will see in the ethnographic reconstructions below, violence acquires a form other than restricted reciprocity and is deployed not simply to retaliate. Violence, actual or threatened, is used to advance over (or protect) a territory for either semilegal commerce (as we saw in chapter 1, as in the case of La Salada where the boundaries of, among other things, stalls and parking lots were defended with gun or knife in hand [Hacher 2011; Girón 2011]) or illegal transactions (as in the monthly, sometimes weekly, shootouts between drug pushers, locally known as *transas*). Physical aggression is also used by parents to discipline sons and daughters, to make them stay away from *malas compañías* (friends deemed bad influences) or, if they "already fell," to try to control their addiction to drugs or alcohol ("Next time I see you with a joint, I'll break your fingers," "He came home so drugged up, I punched him in the face until blood came out of my fingers," or "I chained her to the bed so that she couldn't go out and smoke"). When no other form of punishment works, parents might also resort to the police to have their own children jailed. Physical force (or its threat) is likewise deployed for defense of the self ("I'd kill him with my own bare hands if he tried to rape me" or "Last time my father attacked my mom, she threw a bottle at him and ran him out of the house") or of one's property ("My dad has a gun, he uses it every time intruders want to take a piece of our plot away from us"). Violence, furthermore, is used to obtain economic resources to support drug or alcohol consumption (as in the many robberies by youngsters in the neighborhood: "We ran out of beer and we jumped at this couple to get some money to keep drinking") or dominance over a partner (as in the many domestic fights recounted to us: "He was mad at her because she didn't come back home in time").

These are analytical distinctions that, as we will see, get blurred in daily practice. In other words, there are multiple overlaps between the uses of violence (Hume 2009). A dealer seeks control over his territory in order to conduct his business. In the process he might deploy physical force against youngsters to obtain their silence and protection. The dealer might also use the fact that he is a *poronga pesado* (literally, "a heavy dick," i.e., someone nobody "messes with" in a certain part of the neighborhood) to physically (and publicly) punish an adolescent deemed to be a bad influence on the dealer's daughter. This open, brutal display of physical force against neighbors serves simultaneously to not only discipline family members but also to obtain their respect—and to perpetuate the dealer's reputation. In the examples that follow, we show the mutual imbrication between diverse deployments of violence. The ethnographic reconstructions also illustrate how violence is a routine way to deal with everyday life issues inside and outside the home, that is, physical aggression takes the form of a repertoire of action.

THE SOUNDS OF FEAR

May 16, 2012. Today, sixth grade students discussed a series of short stories about "urban legends" that included ghosts, monsters, and other frightening creatures. "So . . . what are you all afraid of?" Fernanda asks the class. Usually reticent to speak up, the students grab the opportunity to talk about what really matters to them. The question sparks an hour-long conversation about their fears. They say that they are terrified of certain noises. Out of the seven sounds they ask the teacher to write on the blackboard, five concern crime and interpersonal violence: Footsteps on the roof. Rats. Gunshots. Screams during robberies. Clicks of a pistol's trigger and barrel. Storms. And, lastly, one student adds the crackling and explosive blasts of fire because, he says, "When cars are stolen, they burn them and they explode."

Many times, students told us that they could not sleep well because there was a shooting outside, or because "I dreamed that they were breaking into my house . . . in the neighborhood there are always break-ins." Others described how, when hearing shootings or steps on their roofs, they rearranged the furniture, piling everything against the front door so as to prevent a break-in, or how they hid (and sometimes slept) in the only place inside their homes without a window: the bathroom.

"The strength, kind, and structure of the fears and anxieties that smolder or flare in the individual," writes Norbert Elias, "never depend solely on his own 'nature' . . . They are always determined . . . by the history and the actual structure of his relations to other people, by the structure of society; and they change with it" (1994:52). In other words, as Elias would say, the psychogenesis and sociogenesis of fear are two sides of the same coin. The dread expressed by Fernanda's students (and, as we will see, by many adults in the neighborhood) is likewise related to the dangerous relational setting in which they live and, more important, to the uses and forms that violence takes in the neighborhood to which we now turn.

USES AND FORMS

May 17, 2012. "Let's work on the urban legends we read yesterday; let's talk about our fears," Fernanda begins her class. Mario comes to the front and writes on the blackboard: "Get into drugs." "That's what I am scared of," he adds. "The prison," another one states. "Death," two students say in unison. Mario explains: "This is how it goes." He comes back to the blackboard and writes: "Street → bad friends → drugs → prison → death." "It's a chain, miss . . . When you are in the streets, you mess around, you get together with the kids, they make you try drugs, and you like them, and you want more, and you begin to steal to buy drugs. And one day, the cops show up, and they send you to prison. And you stay there four, five, six years, but the cops abuse you. Or they kill you."

For Mario, and for many youngsters and adults with whom we talked during the two and a half years of fieldwork, violence is part of a chain of events, one leading to another. Bad influences forged in the "street" produced a chain reaction that usually led to prison. Although important to understand the way in which residents of Arquitecto Tucci make sense of what is going on there, their notion of "chain" differs from our proposed idea of "concatenation." From our point of view, concatenated violence refers to the many different ways in which diverse types of physical aggression—typically conceptualized as discrete and analytically distinct phenomena (because of the place where they occur, because of the actors involved, etc.)—are in fact linked: an attempted rape followed by a lynching, a dispute between a dealer and a consumer followed by a fight between two brothers, or an attempted robbery followed by a beating inside the household.

Melanie's story, reconstructed below, alerted us to the possible interconnections between forms of violence that, until then, we had thought of as isolated episodes. Research in psychology and community studies reveal the litany of violence to which the poor are subjected and show that different kinds of violence typically "pile up" (Farrell et al. 2007:446; see also Friday 1995). Although many studies highlight the high rates of co-occurrence (between, for example, community violence and interfamilial violence [see, for example, Hume 2009; Wilding 2013]) and demonstrate that exposure to violence seldom takes place in unalloyed ways (Margolin and Gordis 2000; see also, Walton et al. 2009; Korbin 2003; Guerra et al. 2003; Garbarino 1993), our understanding of precisely how different kinds of violence relate to one another in real time and space is quite limited (for exceptions, see Bourgois 1995; LeBlanc 2004). We do not suggest that all violence takes a concatenated form. What we are asserting is that "dyadic retribution" (an eye for an eye) should not exhaust our understanding of violence at the margins. Individual reciprocity is here complemented by interlinkages that only sustained and systematic (i.e., detectivelike) fieldwork can help to unearth.

Melanie's story below signals a change in the empirical focus of our narrative. Thus far, we have largely focused on the frequency of discrete violent episodes (a beating, a shooting, a death) as they appear in the lives of children and adolescents. In what follows, we shift our attention from witnesses and bystanders to the actual perpetrators and direct victims (both young and old) of violence and from isolated incidents to sequences of events.

ON COLLECTIVE RETALIATION

Melanie (eleven) lives in El Bajo, an area of the neighborhood full of precariously constructed homes and meandering passageways. The picture she took of her block vividly reminds the reader of the crumbling infrastructure and polluted environment that people like Melanie experience on a daily basis: dirt roads, open ditches, broken sidewalks, stagnant and stinking sewage waters, and uncollected garbage (see figure 25). Melanie's dad scavenges for a living; her mother is one of the thousands of beneficiaries of the Asignación Universal por Hijo, the Argentine conditional cash transfer program.

The classroom has only one ceiling fan, and it is not working properly. It's really hot inside. Fifteen students are in class today. Melanie and Noelia are sitting together; they are friends and neighbors from El Bajo. Melanie raises her hand and calls Fernanda to her desk. She has not been doing well in school; she missed too many classes. Fernanda approaches her, thinking that Melanie needs further explanation of the assignment. But she is wrong:

MELANIE: Look what happened to me in my leg. I have a bullet, see?

Fernanda looks at her leg and sees she has a scratch but then she notices something like a bump. She asks her what happened.

FIGURE 25. Melanie's street.

MELANIE: It was on Christmas Eve, a stray bullet. I was hanging out on my patio and it happened so suddenly. My neighbors are always firing off guns during Christmas and New Year's. They celebrate.

FERNANDA: Ay, Melanie, that's dangerous. And how are you?

MELANIE: I'm okay. I went to the hospital and now it's okay. It's nothing. They are not going to take the bullet out. I don't know why.

Melanie, as it turns out, is not telling Fernanda the entire truth about the origin of the bullet. A few hours later, Mabel, Melanie's mother, comes to pick her up. She is all sweaty when Fernanda meets her; it's a very long walk from El Bajo to the school, and she is carrying her two-week-old baby, Franco, in her arms. She sits down in one of the classroom chairs, visibly tired. While Mabel breast-feeds Franco, Fernanda mentions Melanie's accident and tells Mabel how terrible she imagines it must have been to spend Christmas in the hospital, all because of a stray bullet. Mabel then launches into a monologue that depicts a prominent form of violence affecting young girls in the neighborhood and a form of communal (re)action to it.

> MABEL: See, that son of a bitch wanted to rape her. It was on December 24. We have a big family, so we had asked a neighbor to roast a pig and some chickens. This is a neighbor I've known all my life. My brother-in-law brought home the pig, but there were some chickens missing, so I sent Melanie and my niece to pick them up. When they got to the neighbor's house, he wanted to rape them. He was drunk, and had a knife in his hand. And he told Melanie and my niece that if they didn't suck his dick, he was going to kill one, and then rape and kill the other one. Luckily, they were able to push him aside—maybe because he was really smashed—and they escaped. They ran home and told us what had just happened. My husband, my brothers-in-law, my brother, and some other neighbors went to his house and beat the shit out of him [*lo recagaron a palos*]. They beat his face to a pulp; he was full of blood. They left him there, lying on the floor, and came back home. After dinner, around midnight, that son of a bitch came to my house and shot at Melanie. Luckily, the bullet hit her in the leg. All the men in my house went back to his house and beat the shit out of him again. I had to run to the [state] hospital [located 30 minutes away]. I spent the night of the 24th and the 25th there. They checked her out very well, to see if she had been raped. Luckily, the guy didn't get to do anything to her.

As Mabel recounts the events of that night—her voice never wavering—Melanie listens attentively. Fernanda can't shake her shock at Mabel's story and asks her about the whereabouts of her neighbor-predator.

FERNANDA: Did you call the police?

MABEL: No, we didn't call the police. That son of a bitch left the neighborhood; he went to [the province of] Corrientes. I can assure you he will not be back.

Dozens of times over the course of our fieldwork, we heard stories of rape or attempted rape of girls by acquaintances or family members—in most of the cases, uncles or stepfathers. Over the course of individual interviews, parents articulate their fear: "I can't let her go alone . . . what if they rape her? It's frightening." Despite this panic—a panic with a very real basis—neighbors like Mabel do not trust the police to address these kinds of cases. They think cops are slow in reacting against sexual violence ("the police always come late, to collect the body if someone was killed, or to stitch you up if you were raped") and/or complicit with it (rumors about the existence of what a neighbor calls "the blow-job police"—that is, cops who demand sexual favors from neighborhood adolescents—run rampant).[3] Residents thus rarely rely on a legal charge (and a possible arrest). Instead they often deploy targeted, retaliatory collective violence. Yet, as we will see in chapter 4, collective retaliation is one type of response among many to the violence that surrounds and permeates daily life in Tucci. For now, we will concentrate on the interconnected character of forms of violence to which Melanie's story first alerted us. This concatenated character is further illustrated in the ethnographic vignettes that follow.

FUZZY BOUNDARIES

Reconstructed over a period of several days, and after long and difficult conversations with some of the participants involved, the following episode begins to illustrate the porous boundaries between private and public violence, as well as the diverse uses of physical aggression that characterize violence as a local repertoire of action.[4]

Lucía and her friend Soledad are both thirteen years old. They live on the same block. Lucía's mother, Matilde, is a single mother. Soledad's father, Juan, is a well-known drug dealer in this area of the neighborhood, *un poronga pesado* (someone "nobody messes with"). Soledad's mom, Rosario, also has a reputation for being tough. As a neighbor told us, "He is a *transa* [drug dealer], and he is loaded with guns and has no problems if he has to shoot at someone. And his wife, I worked with her [robbing trucks going in and out of the street market], and I know what she is capable of doing."

One Monday morning in early September 2011, neighbors awoke to the sounds of Juan's and Rosario's screams. "She [Soledad] was raped because of you [Lucía]! You will see!" Right after publicly and loudly accusing Lucía for their daughter's misfortune, they grabbed her by the arms, punched her in the face, and kicked her in her stomach and lower back. Then they pulled her inside their home. Inside, Juan held her firmly while Rosario swiftly cut her long hair. Lucía sprinted back to her house. When Matilde heard Lucía frantically crying under her bed, curled up in the fetal position, she ran out to the sidewalk to see what had happened. Outside, she was confronted by Rosario and Juan: "You better keep this to yourself or you'll be in trouble," they told her. Amanda, Matilde's friend, later told us that she believes that Matilde has no way to counter the couple's brutality toward her daughter: "She can't do anything. If she says something, they'll kill her."

Everybody on the block talked about the public punishment, but the offense was not immediately obvious. What happened? Why did Juan and Rosario publicly and viciously scold Lucía? It took us a while to find out. That morning, Lucía and Soledad had come back home at 6:00 a.m. after spending the night out with no more than a single phone call to their parents to tell them they were "on their way [home]." When they showed up in the morning, Soledad's neck was "filled with *chupones* [hickies]." It didn't take long for Juan and Rosario to realize that their daughter had had sex and, equating a first-time sexual encounter with rape, they blamed her friend Lucía for the loss of their daughter's virginity—though, as Matilde confided to us later, "Soledad was no virgin, no way." The equivalence between a first sexual encounter and rape is not, we believe, far-fetched. Given Soledad's age and the widespread fear of sexual violence in the neighborhood, the dreadful comparison makes sense.

"Lucía didn't force Soledad to do anything she didn't want to," Matilde told us. But Juan and Rosario blamed Lucía for their daughter's condition—the attribution of blame took the form of harsh physical punishment carried out by those who see themselves as the de facto authority in this part of the neighborhood. Juan and Rosario are not alone in believing that, *pace* Hannah Arendt, power can come out of "the barrel of a gun"—or a punch, a knife, or a stick. Violence, in many a resident's view, does not "destroy power" (Arendt 1970) but actually gives birth to (and/or sustains) it. Violence is, for many in the area, foundational. It nurtures the power a man or a woman can hold both inside and outside his or her home, serving both disciplinary and reputational purposes. In both private and public spheres, authority is (thought to be) conquered and defended with physical violence— "Grab a stick, or a pipe," Amanda offered, as parental advice to Matilde, "and hit him [your son] hard with it, until he listens to you, until he obeys you. That's the only way in which he is going to comply." "You will learn a lesson," screamed Soledad's parents at Lucía as they punched and kicked her adolescent body.

The following two reconstructions exemplify other ways in which different forms of interpersonal violence are connected. Regularly performed, violence takes the form of a useful repertoire to deal with routine problems at the urban margins.

USING VIOLENCE

We first heard about Leonardo when his mother, Ana, approached Agustín at the soup kitchen. Knowing that Agustín had helped another neighbor place her addicted son into a rehabilitation center, Ana sought his help. "Please, give me a hand with this; I can't take it anymore." Earlier that morning, Ana had beaten Leonardo "with the broom. I hit him everywhere, arms, legs . . . I lost it," she says, crying. "I swear to you, I lost it. I didn't want to stop beating him until I could see blood coming out."

It took us several weeks to reconstruct the story behind the beating. Agustín spent time with Ana and Leonardo in the precarious exposed-brick one-room home they inhabit. He chatted with Ana as she cooked lunch for dozens in the soup kitchen, which she joined, as did many of the women who work there, to escape from her abusive husband. And he visited a rehab center (a one-and-a-half-hour train and bus ride from the neighborhood) together with Leonardo, after he expressed his desire to "rescue" himself from drugs.

Leonardo, who is now sixteen, dropped out of school when he was fourteen, and has been consuming paco for at least two years. He also drinks heavily ("oftentimes, I get drunk, I get into fights, but then I don't remember a thing . . . I wake up full of scars and don't remember anything"). He has been financing his harmful habits by scavenging, robbing inside and outside the neighborhood (which triggered several altercations with the police and one arrest), and stealing from his mother.

Three times a week, Leonardo scavenges around the neighborhood with a cart—"I don't have a horse, so I can't go far," he tells Agustín. As do many others, he combines this informal labor with illicit activities like robbing from passersby and from local stores. "I began to rob when I was twelve, with a kid that now is a drug pusher [*transa*]. We used to cut school . . . at the beginning I was really scared. We would go walk around the store [we wanted to rob] or get close to the person we wanted to mug, but we wouldn't dare do it. You have to go with someone else, so that you get the courage [*así te das fuerza*]. If not, if you go alone, you get frightened, and you don't rob anyone."

The "seductions of crime" (Katz 1988) were not only learned in the company of his partners. Leonardo's older half brother, Matías, acted as a "role model" of sorts. Although Leonardo never "went out [to commit a crime] with him," he remembers "him coming home from work [a robbery] . . . taking off his [bulletproof] vest, and leaving his guns in the top drawer, where I couldn't reach . . . he would then lock it so that I couldn't get my hands on his guns." Leonardo respected and admired Matías. Matías was a thief, a *chorro*. In the symbolic universe of these poor, destitute, delinquent youth, thieves have the moral upper hand over *transas*.[5]

Robbing from stores in the neighborhood is "difficult," says Leonardo, not only because many "storeowners are armed . . . even more so if they are men," but also because of the police. Together with his partner, Quito, he was arrested when trying to rob a grocery store in nearby Villa Itatí. They were placed in a detention center for minors for a few months. Leonardo has a scar on his cheek, a daily reminder of that arrest ("they stepped on my face and held it to the ground . . . there must have been a stone or glass there and it punctured my skin"). Violence is also inscribed on his body in the form of several tattoos: A black .22 mm pistol ("you can distinguish it from a .38 mm by the cylinder and the barrel") on his chest surrounded by wings on each side, and five dots (four dots, representing inmates or thieves, surrounding one that represents a cop) on his right leg ("if the cops see this tattoo, they take you to the precinct, and they beat the shit out of you, even if you haven't done anything," he proudly states). On his right arm, he has tattooed his seventeen-year-old sister's name, Dalma. Dalma was arrested while carrying one kilogram of pure cocaine. After months of detention without sentence,[6] she was released—but not before having been raped behind bars, apparently contracting HIV.

"He has stolen everything from me," says Leonardo's mother, Ana. "We can't live with him anymore." She elaborates: "Leonardo has stolen many things from me. The first time I beat him was when he sold a cell phone he stole from us. The cell phone wasn't even mine; it was from my second husband. I beat him really bad; I grabbed his fingers and told him that if he did that again, I was going to break his fingers, one by one, so that he couldn't steal again. He never took a cell phone again, but he stole sneakers, T-shirts, socks. I buy stuff at the feria [La Salada] so that I can resell it and make some money [but] he steals it from me and resells it for twenty pesos so that he can buy his drugs."

Ana beat Leonardo out of impotence but also out of fear. She is afraid her son will be killed. Examples of early, violent deaths abound around them. Leonardo's idolized half brother, Matías, was killed (nobody knows by whom) in an attempted robbery a few months before we met (his half-dead body was abandoned, presumably by his partners in crime, in front of the local hospital). This loss, according to Ana, intensified Leonardo's paco consumption (in Leonardo's words, "since what happened to my brother, I really abandoned myself"). Weeks before we first met, Leonardo was hit by a bullet in his leg when he and a group of friends tried to mug a passerby in the middle of the night. Daniel, the brother of Leonardo's friend Kevin (with whom Leonardo consumes drugs), was killed in that encounter. As Leonardo told us, "The guy [we were going to mug] pulled out his own gun and began to shoot. I started to run. I hid in an abandoned house, and realized my leg was injured." It was the first time Leonardo was hit by a bullet. Ana fears that her losing control over him will result in him being killed ("Last night, he came back home high, drugged, aggressive. He still obeys me and he has not tried to hit me yet, but the friend with whom he does drugs [Kevin] does not even respect his mother; he is out of control"). Late one afternoon, as Agustín, Ana, and Leonardo were watching Argentina play Bolivia on TV in a qualifying round for the World Cup, she articulated this fear:

LEONARDO: My mother never leaves me alone.

AGUSTÍN: Leonardo, she is doing that because she is worried.

ANA: Son, I'm very worried. In the same way you have trouble breathing when you are not well, my heart speeds up when I think that someone may kill you.

LEONARDO: If she were worried, she wouldn't hit me.

AGUSTÍN: It's not that she enjoys beating you, come on. She does it out of impotence. She doesn't know what to do with you.

ANA: I don't know what to do so that you react!

Earlier that week, as the plans to place Leonardo into a rehab center for minors were taking shape (Agustín had developed a good working relationship with the center's director), Ana expressed doubts about the internment: "I don't know . . . because, although I sometimes have to hit him, he still obeys me, he never screams at me, he never tried to hit me back. When I beat him, he lets it go, he barely protects himself, and he doesn't complain. I still have control over him . . . But yes, I guess I want to put him into a rehab clinic . . . so that he recovers, so that nothing bad happens to him. What if he is the next one to die? I'm really anguished. When he comes back drugged, I can't do anything else other than beat him, because he doesn't understand me, because I've spoken to him and he never listens. And I don't want to hit him anymore, for him, for me, for my daughters who see everything."

As many in the neighborhood, Ana and Leonardo are quite familiar with crime and violence. Ana herself had been a drug pusher for a while ("but I didn't make much money because I did drugs too"). Ana's first husband, Mario (Leonardo's and Dalma's dad), was a drug dealer "a *transa pesado* . . . a big fish, he had lots of money," she tells us. Her second husband, Roberto (the father of Leonardo's sisters, Florencia, fifteen; Laura, nine; and Roxana, seven), was a part-time thief: "He used to rob on the highway every now and then, but he was no big fish, no *pirata del asfalto* [literally, not an "asphalt pirate"] . . . [He committed] small robberies . . . a cell phone, a wallet with a hundred pesos, nothing big . . . he was even afraid of my first husband. Now, my first husband, yes, that man was scary." Mario was not only a "scary" thug; he was also a menacing husband. "He used to beat me very, very often . . . He once chopped my hair this short [pointing to above her ear]. He not only beat the shit out of me, he also starved me . . . Why do you think I began to work at the soup kitchen? They didn't pay me but I got food there . . . he made my life hell. When I became pregnant with Florencia, he beat me really hard. And she wasn't even his daughter, we were no longer together. But all the same, he wanted me to have an abortion, he punched me several times in my belly, screaming, 'take that girl out of there, get rid of her!'" Leonardo remembers these fights: "Once, he almost killed her. When I was a kid, I swore I'd murder my father."

The day Leonardo had his appointment with the counselor at the local health center (so that she could do a "psychological evaluation," which would authorize his admission to rehab), he was nowhere to be found. Despite his declared desire to *rescatarse de las drogas* (quit consuming), he missed the one chance he had to get free treatment. Ana did not see him until a few days later when he, drunk or high (Ana couldn't tell), tried to break into her house. He was "out of control," Ana told Agustín. "He came home, and when I was about to beat him, he yelled, 'Now you will see who is Leonardo Jesús Ramírez. The Leonardo who was told what to do, that Leonardo is gone! From now on, I'll do whatever the fuck I want, and if I die, I die *en mi ley* [by my law]!'"

Later that day, Ana found out that Leonardo had had a fight with his partner, Roxana. Leonardo had read a text message Roxana had received from a former boyfriend while she was taking a shower and, in a jealous outburst, beat her so badly that she had to be hospitalized. Feeling worthless (his male pride threatened), Leonardo went ballistic on the person closest to him. No authority intervened—Leonardo was not cited or arrested for the episode. All Ana could say when we last saw her was, "Believe me, Agustín, I know how it feels when somebody beats the shit out of you."

Exposure to violence(s), the above story shows, comes in diverse forms: direct victimization, witnessing, or learning about physical harm perpetrated against others (Brennan et al. 2007). But the narrative also reveals that violence is regularly deployed to accomplish a variety of aims, and that some of these uses concatenate with one another. The next ethnographic reconstruction illuminates these concatenations in greater empirical detail, shedding light on the dissemination of violent interactions beyond the confines of one-on-one reciprocity.

DRUGS AND VIOLENCE

Angélica (forty-five) lives in a precarious house made of bricks, wood, and metal sheets for a roof. The house bears the marks of her son Antonio's (seventeen) addiction to paco. A

FIGURE 26. El Checho's.

big wood panel covers a hole Antonio made when, in desperate need of cash to buy his next dose of paco, he broke into his own house and stole Angélica's clothes. Clothes are not the only thing that Antonio has stolen from his mother and siblings. The list, Angélica tells us, is quite long. It includes a TV set, brand-new sneakers, plates, pots, pans, and a new portable washing machine.

Just a few blocks from their house there is a shop (El Checho's; figure 26) that specializes in buying items from desperate addicts and then resells them to either their original owners or anyone interested for a higher, oftentimes doubled, price. These days Angélica seldom leaves the house (she stopped taking her little son to day care, and she failed to show up at the local hospital to give her two little children mandatory vaccines), because she is afraid Antonio will take whatever items of value remain—"the little TV antenna . . . he broke it, he uses it as a pipe to smoke." But Antonio doesn't just steal from Angélica. Recently he has begun to take clothes from one of her other sons, Carlos. Carlos is an alcoholic, and last time he discovered Antonio's robberies, a huge bloody fight broke out between them. "They threw rocks and bottles at each other," Angélica tells us. And many of her neighbors agree; the fights between the two sick brothers are infamous on their block. Impotent, but hardly passive in the face of that violence (many times we witnessed how Angélica makes sure that there are no glass bottles or big rocks handy in their backyard so that the brothers cannot severely hurt each other), she is very scared (*vivo con miedo*) at the prospect of one of them killing the other. In the following dialogue, Angélica recounts one recent episode.

ANGÉLICA: Antonio spent last night in the precinct.

AGUSTÍN: What happened?

ANGÉLICA: He stole our bathroom's toilet . . . and when he was carrying it through the streets, the police stopped him. The cops thought he had stolen it from a local depot. They arrested him.

AGUSTÍN: Did you at least get the toilet back?

ANGÉLICA: No . . . I don't have the money to bring it back from the precinct [she needs to pay a car service]. And that's not all. Carlos beat Antonio really bad for stealing the toilet. Today, in vengeance, Antonio threw a huge paving stone at his foot, to hurt him.

AGUSTÍN: How did Antonio do that? Was Carlos asleep?

ANGÉLICA: Carlos has been drunk for the past three days, drinking wine, beer, and whiskey . . . [*crying*] My life is not a life . . . Sometimes, I want to leave them all here and run away.

Violence between the drug-addicted son and the alcoholic one is not the only violence that threatens Angélica's household, where seven other children, ranging from four to twenty-one, live with her. "I couldn't sleep yesterday," she tells us as we are walking toward the local soup kitchen on a Friday morning. "Antonio stole a bicycle from a neighbor, who is a friend of Carlos. Antonio exchanged it for twenty pesos to buy drugs. At night, the owner of the bicycle came to my home and asked me for the bicycle. I told him that I'd get paid on Tuesday. But he doesn't want the money. He showed me a gun and told me that, 'if the bicycle is not here soon, I'll kill your son.'" Angélica and the rest of her family didn't sleep that night. Antonio and Carlos do not fight only over the items the first steals from the second. Carlos also blames Antonio for putting everybody in danger. After the neighbor threatened to kill Antonio over the missing bicycle, Carlos worried out loud: "I'm scared; that guy is capable of anything."

Antonio is not only addicted to paco but, lately, he has also been purchasing drugs for other youngsters in the neighborhood, acting as a courier of sorts. One night a group of youth angrily stormed into Angélica's house looking for Antonio. They had given him money earlier in the day, and by late afternoon he had not returned with the drugs (or the money). "They looked for him everywhere and they had weapons," Angélica said. "They threatened me and told me that they would kill him because he had kept their money. I told them that I'd pay them. I told them that he didn't know what he was doing. I asked them to please not hurt him."

The constant—and, as far as we were able to see, increasingly dangerous—fights between residents can, in part, be understood as the psychopharmacological product of the consumption of drugs and alcohol. As research has shown (Reinarman and Levine 1997; Parker and Auerhahn 1998), the ingestion of alcohol and drugs can irritate, excite, enrage, or embolden people; these emotional states can translate into violent behavior. Antonio's petty thievery, compelled by his craving for drugs, illustrates yet another individual-level relationship between drugs and violence—what Paul Goldstein (1985) labels "economic compulsive" (see also Goldstein et al. 1997).

Until the proliferation of crack use in the United States, most research attributed the violence triggered by drugs either to "the physical or psychological effects of drug ingestion or to the attempts of drug addicts to acquire economic resources that are needed to support the habit" (Ousey and Lee 2002:74–75). Since the mid-1980s, research has uncovered a third way in which drugs and violence are coupled. Systemic violence refers to the violence that can develop "from the exigencies of working or doing business in an illicit market—a context in which the monetary stakes can be enormous but where the economic actors have no recourse to the legal system to resolve disputes" (Goldstein 1985:116). In this third way, which accounts for most of what is known as "drug-related" violence, violent interactions are "an outcome of attempts at informal social control carried out by drug market participants who are unable to rely on formal social control agents (e.g., the police) to handle their grievances" (Ousey and Lee 2002:75). Disputes between rival dealers, punishment for stealing or failing to pay for drugs, or for selling adulterated products, are commonly cited examples (Reinarman and Levine 1997; Ousey and Lee 2002; Bourgois 1995; Venkatesh 2008; Reding 2009). Angélica's family also had firsthand experience with this violence, and so do many of Fernanda's students, as attested to by the many times in which they report night shootouts between neighborhood drug dealers: "In the neighborhood, every night, dealers shoot at each other."

The above story illustrates more than the coexistence, in real time and space, of the three forms in which drugs and violence are related. When, in his attempt to finance his habit and/or pay back his debts, Antonio steals from his family members and ends up in a fight with his brother, or when young addicts terrorize Angélica and her family over missing drugs, we also see how reciprocity diffuses and violence is used for many purposes other than retaliation (to obtain economic resources, to discipline, etc.). Diverse forms of violence that have traditionally been examined as separate and distinct phenomena (e.g., interpersonal, domestic, drug-related) connect with one another. As drug dealers, couriers, and consumers fight over payments, theft, or drug quality, their public violence—a violence that is inherent to the structure of the market for illicit goods—may migrate inside homes and become a private, sometimes brutal, quarrel between family members.

Many an episode of violence that, on first appearance, seems discrete and self-contained is—as the stories of Melanie, Leonardo, Ana, Antonio, and Angélica show—part of a sequence of concatenated events. Different forms of violence not only coexist (Walton et al. 2009; Korbin 2003; Hume 2009) but also interlink with one another. In doing so, the boundaries between street and home, between public and domestic, become blurred.

Part of the "why" so much violence exists is in the "how" residents at the urban margins use physical aggression. Violence, in contemporary Arquitecto Tucci, as in many other times and places, is deployed to build or maintain authority inside the home, and to shape reputations in the neighborhood. These uses, needless to say, bolster particular conceptions of respect and domination centered on the deployment of physical force as an instrument, and contribute to the reproduction of social hierarchies.

An attentive reading of the reconstructions above reveals that violence is also used to solve (or to attempt to solve) individual and collective problems (from obtaining resources to finance a habit or protecting property to controlling a wayward adolescent son or daughter or punishing a predator). Regularly performed in a variety of instances, violence takes the form of a repertoire of action that serves to address a diversity of daily difficulties. Conceptualizing violence as a repertoire leads us to not only identify regularities in individual and collective deployments of physical force (the task of this chapter) but also to examine, in true Tillyan fashion (1986; 1995), its political dimensions. When confronted with such levels of violence, we should ask who—if anyone—is policing these interpersonal disputes and, relatedly, why residents rarely seek the intervention of the organization that presumably monopolizes the use of force: the state. Such an intervention, a close reading of the material presented above should note, may not have prevented every violent interaction but could have interrupted its escalation and concatenation with other forms. In part, residents do not rely on state agents (e.g., municipal officials, school counselors, police officers, therapists at drug rehab clinics) because they are often nowhere to be found. But they also avoid the state and its representatives out of mistrust, as hinted at in the rumors about the "blow-job police." However, a comprehensive account of the state presence in the area should go beyond the tropes of "absence" and "mistrust." Such is the task we have undertaken in chapter 3.

CHAPTER 3

THE STATE AT THE MARGINS

In *The Civilizing Process* (1994), Norbert Elias posits the existence of a mutually reinforcing relationship between the pacification of daily life in a given region and the actions (or inactions) of the state that rules over that area. The "civilizing process" means, above all, the removal of violence from social life and its relocation under the control of the state. Elias's insight is particularly pertinent to understanding and explaining the diverse forms of criminal and interpersonal violence that are ravaging Tucci residents' lives. Taking heed of Elias's general proposition, and confronted with the intensification of urban violence in the area, we should ask: When, how, and to what effect does the state police this place?

In this chapter we examine the relationship between the state's presence at the urban margins and the depacification of poor people's daily lives in Tucci. Contrary to descriptions of destitute urban areas in the Americas as either "governance voids" deserted by the state (Anderson 1999; Koonings and Kruijt 2007; Venkatesh 2008) or militarized spaces firmly controlled by the state's iron fist (Müller 2011; Rios 2010), we argue that law enforcement in Arquitecto Tucci is—analogous to the forms of governance analyzed by Dennis Rodgers in Managua's barrios (2006) and by Desmond Arias in Rio de Janeiro's favelas (2006)—*intermittent, selective,* and *contradictory.* By putting the state's fractured presence at the urban margins under the ethnographic microscope, we reveal its key role in the perpetuation of the violence it is presumed to prevent.

As we stated in the introduction, social scientific and journalistic descriptions of violence in marginalized urban territories abound in the Americas (Alarcón 2009; Anderson 1999; Aricapa 2005; Castillo Berthier and Jones 2009; Friday 1995; Gay 2005; Goldstein 2003, 1998; Harding 2010; Jones 2009; Venkatesh 2008; Wilding 2010). However, notwithstanding recent detailed accounts (Goldstein 2012; Rodgers 2006), we know preciously little about the ways in which the actions or inactions of state agents may tame or increase this violence. Based on fieldwork in the neighborhood and its police station, this chapter seeks to fill this void.

As should be clear by now, collective life in Arquitecto Tucci is anything but peaceful. Violence abounds in the social spaces in which residents, young and old, interact daily. It is experienced, witnessed, or talked about in homes, schools, and the streets. In the face of violence that is neither tamed nor "behind the scenes" (Elias 1978), we ask, together with Elias, how does the state intervene? The state is both an abstract, macrolevel structure and a concrete, microlevel set of institutions with which the urban poor interact in direct and immediate ways. In this chapter we concentrate on the latter, the level of *state practice* (Gupta 2005; Haney 1996; Secor 2007), by focusing on residents' routine, but not always licit, encounters with law enforcement officials and on both residents' and police agents' viewpoints on violence in the area.

As stated in chapter 1, the area where we conducted our fieldwork sits adjacent to the biggest street fair in the country.

FIGURE 27. Guarding La Salada.

As described above, twice a week, thousands of shoppers (mostly from lower and lower-middle classes from metropolitan Buenos Aires but also traders from the rest of the country) come to its markets to purchase mostly apparel and small electronics. Because of the La Salada street fair, hundreds of thousands of pesos in cash and merchandise pass through the streets of Arquitecto Tucci each week, providing excellent opportunities for street crime. As described in chapter 1, together with the market's private security forces, military-style federal forces, known as the National Guard (Gendarmería Nacional), patrol the streets hours before and during these *días de feria*. Numerous and heavily armed with state-of-the-art equipment, the imposing presence of private guards and federal soldiers transforms the area into a militarized space. In certain areas surrounding the feria, private security guards and the gendarmes create *cordones* (passageways) through which shoppers and merchants come in and out of the fair (figure 27).

But this militarization of marginality (Müller 2011; Wacquant 2008) does not last for long—once the markets close, the gendarmes and the private guards disappear until the fair's next opening. The poorly paid, trained, and equipped state police (known as La Bonaerense) patrol the streets when the National Guard is gone.

Thirty months of observation, and innumerable conversations with residents young and old, reveal the highly skewed and contradictory character of this intermittent law enforcement. Before documenting this pernicious state presence, let us present a brief account of the ways in which the local police see the area and its residents. What they say is important not because it describes the actual nature of police intervention in the area—it does not—but because it hints at a variation of what Scheper-Hughes (1992) calls the state's "averted gaze," in this case, permeated by an ethnicized (mis)understanding of local violence.

The View from the Precinct

The whiteboard filled with month-by-month figures of homicides, assaults, robberies, car thefts, and rapes gives the impression that the local police office closely follows the ups and downs of crime in the area.[1] But, as we talk to the district chief, we realize these figures should be taken with caution. It is the beginning of March 2013 and the whiteboard has not been updated for two months. "We used a permanent marker . . . and, well, we can't erase it now. We are waiting for a new whiteboard." Figures for January and February are nowhere to be found, but the district chief assures us that "he knows them by heart." A few weeks later, we interviewed a federal police officer who works in the area, and who, since the murder of her brother (according to her account, by a gang composed of common criminals and members of the state police), has been acting as a sort of whistleblower of police force corruption. In no uncertain terms, she told us: "The figures are lies" (*las cifras se mienten*).

Crime statistics are certainly not the only figures that are either made up or badly recorded in the area; hospitals and schools are not very diligent at record keeping either. The seemingly anecdotal episode of the permanent marker would certainly appear to indicate a state that has turned away from the problems of crime and violence that affect the area. But a careful reconstruction of the point of view of local police agents shows that they are far from indifferent. Although inaccurate, their understandings are highly relevant for what they say (and what they hide) about their collective attempt to define the origins and dynamics of interpersonal violence in the area.

"Complex," "different," "complicated," and "very particular" are the words the police agents at the local precinct use to describe Arquitecto Tucci. "It is something that you don't see in many other places," says the district chief, and then, in a statement that summarizes the opinions of the seven interviewed agents, adds, "In a small area, you have a huge population, and you have many, many [ethnic] communities [*colectividades*]. Tucci also has a special 'seasoning' that is the famous fair of La Salada, which brings more than fifty thousand people every time it opens its doors." Although some of them use, as we will see, less euphemized forms to talk about residents and their behavior, they all agree—in what resembles a monolithic point of view—on the main reasons behind Tucci's complexity and unique character: it is crowded, it is "filled with foreigners," and the largest informal market in the country (which every time it opens "brings a number of people that equals the number that attend a big soccer match") operates within its territorial boundaries.

Interestingly, the same factors that describe the neighborhood's particularity are the ones that, from the precinct's point of view, explain the violence in the area. Note how two agents, who are in charge of the office on gender violence, depict the neighborhood, its residents, and its violence:

AGENT 1: It's all very different here . . . starting with the aroma. When you come here from other places, such as [middle-class districts of] Lomas or Llavallol, you first wonder: "What am I doing here?" You are used to good smells, you are used to presentable, personable folks; people who say "please." People here come to the office and start fighting.

FLORENCIA (*interviewer*): And where do you think those differences come from?

AGENT 2: It is wrong to be racist or to discriminate. But most people who live here . . . most are foreigners. And most are like that.

Statements like the above should not be discarded as outliers. These gross stereotypes resonate among other members of the force, including the district chief. While trying to explain the recent increase in homicides, he comes back to the community's ethnic composition: "Here you have many communities, Peruvians, Paraguayans, Bolivians." Violence is "cultural . . . that's how they are; they kill each other [*se matan entre ellos*]. Take the case of Bolivians. They kill each other because they have economic differences, or because of jealousy, or simply because of beefs they have among themselves. There is a lot of violence because Paraguayans and Bolivians drink too much. They drink from dusk to dawn. After all the drinking, they don't know what they have done, they don't remember anything." Violence, according to local agents, comes from outside(rs); those who commit acts of violence are "people coming from other places." Foreigners not only bring the violence into Arquitecto Tucci, they also make police work more difficult: "Bolivians, Peruvians, and Paraguayans are too reserved [*son muy cerrados*]. The Paraguayans, for example, speak in Guaraní, and it's too difficult to investigate [the crimes]. They are too reserved. It is very difficult to work here." Difficulties in combating crime are compounded by another—and, according to agents, equally pernicious—element: these days, people "know their rights." As another agent puts it, "Youth know their rights now. Before, if you saw them loitering on the street corner, you asked for their IDs and sent them home. Nowadays, you can't do that [because] they know their rights . . . You can't do anything if you see them smoking a joint, because it is now allowed."[2]

Police agents understand the origins and character of violence as "cultural." Violence is "cultural" because it is related to the national origins of the foreign populations in Tucci, to their (ethnic) ways of doing things, to their cultural "way of being" (*su forma de ser*). But the local police point of view on the widespread violence is not without its critics. Without even knowing we would also interview the district chief, the federal police officer mentioned at the beginning of this section anticipated what we would hear from him, and provided a straightforward critique: "The police chief is going to tell you that the people in Tucci are killing each other because they are *cabezas negras* . . . and that is not true.[3] There is a lot of crime, because there are a lot of drugs . . . and things are much more complicated. The cops are in cahoots with the criminals."

As we described in chapter 1, it is certainly true that the street fair brings a "special seasoning" to the area, not only in terms of the number of people it brings weekly, but also in terms of the opportunities for crime it presents (or, as the police chief puts it, "When the fair is closed, Tucci is a normal neighborhood"). But Arquitecto Tucci's total population is nowhere close to the 500,000 the district chief believes it to be (neither has it grown 300 percent in the last ten years, as he states). The majority of its residents, contrary to what agents think, are from Argentina. At odds with the view from the precinct, furthermore, violent crime has no ethnonational dimension. According to information published in the local newspapers (and confirmed by the Supreme Court's report on 2012 homicides), a really small percentage of the murders committed in the area during 2009–12 were perpetrated by a foreigner. Criminal violence and the kinds of interpersonal disputes mentioned by the police officials are unequivocally unrelated to "culture."

Although highly biased and mistaken on many grounds, we must take seriously the view from the precinct because it reinforces the erroneous belief that Arquitecto Tucci is a particular place because it

has all the wrong "ingredients," whose very constitu-
tion determines its high levels of violence. By in-
venting and stressing the "cultural" character of the
violence in the area, the precinct view disguises the
political underpinning (including police complicity)
of local violence, which, as we will now see, is crucial
to understanding its dynamics.

The daily interpersonal violence that overwhelms residents
confirms, to both victims and perpetrators, that the place
where they live exists as a stigmatized and stigmatizing region,
literally, a relegated territory, that is, removed and subordinated.[4] Or, as one neighbor eloquently puts it, "It hurts when
I hear people saying that Tucci is a 'red zone.' A lot of people
who look for jobs or sign up for a course deny that they live in
Tucci; they fill their applications stating that they live in
Lomas de Zamora [the district to which Tucci belongs]. Because if you say you are from here, they brand you as a bad
person. That hurts. There are many bad things here, but there's
also a lot of good people, working folks." Residents also believe
that their neighborhood is a place that "nobody seems to care
about," where "anything goes" because it is "liberated" from
state intervention.[5] In what follows we turn to this subject by
relying on a series of vignettes to depict the particular presence
of the repressive arm of the state in the area. We will see how
the state contradicts itself when simultaneously implementing
and breaking the rules it has itself created.

THE COP'S SON

Julián (thirteen) is in sixth grade, and his father is a policeman who works for La Bonaerense. During the first recess, he
asks Fernanda to hold his brand-new, high-tech cell phone
while he runs around the playground with his friends. Fer-

nanda has only seen them on TV and praises the object, "What a nice cell phone you've got!" He replies, "My father gave it to me. He took it away from the thieves. Have you seen when the cops put the thieves against the wall and pat them? Well, that's when my dad takes away their cell phones, money, drugs . . . he never returns them. He keeps everything for himself. And he gave this one [pointing to the new cell phone] to me as a present. It's nice, isn't it?" The natural, unaffected way in which Julián told Fernanda about the cell phone's origins suggests that he believes that there is nothing wrong with his father's actions; but this is not the place to speculate about the kind of moral lesson learned by Julián every time he hears about and benefits from his dad's exploits. We are concerned not with the crafting of a child's moral judgment but with what the story can tell us about the contradictory ways in which the state appears in poor people's lives. Julián's story points toward one prominent way in which law enforcement operates in the neighborhood: the police act as the repressive arm of the state against criminals but also as the perpetrators of crime; police agents uphold the rule of law and simultaneously break it. This is hardly a secret for Fernanda's students and the adult residents with whom we talked. As they repeatedly state, "They [the cops] are all addicts [*drogones*]"; "They [the cops] are all thieves [*chorros*]."

Tucci residents are not alone in this belief. In a perceptive and detailed ethnographic account of shantytown life in Quilmes, another municipality in the southern sector of Greater Buenos Aires, anthropologist Nathalie Puex examines shanty-dwellers' perceptions of the connection between criminal and police activity, as well as the linkages between shanty youngsters and authorities:

> For many shantytown residents [*villeros*] the cop is another thief [*chorro*] . . . The police officer does not repre-

sent the law because he himself takes part in criminal activity. [This participation creates an] image of the police as both a repressive force and a provider of jobs. Most of the young delinquents in the shantytown "work" for the police; in other words, they are part of an illicit organization directed by policemen who offer work to these shanty youngsters. Many of these youngsters obtain their income through participating in this organization. (2003:66)[6]

In an interview at the Patronato de Liberados (the state office in charge of the residents recently released from prison or under the supervision of the penal system), state agents confirm that the illicit links between police agents and young delinquents spotted by Puex also operate in Tucci. Police agents recruit youngsters recently released from prison (and on probation) for illegal activities (car theft, for example). These youths do not have many options other than to accept the devil's bargain; otherwise, the cops make up a case against them and they will have to return to prison.

The following two vignettes provide further evidence of the mutual imbrication between criminal activity and state action as experienced at the ground level by the poor residents of Arquitecto Tucci.

THE CAR THIEF

"At that time," says Amelia, referring to the late 1990s and early 2000s, "there were not many things a single mother with three kids and no job could do. I've done everything: stealing cars, selling drugs, robbing people in the streets . . . you name it, I did everything." Pointing at the different Tramontina knives that hang from the wall of her kitchen, she then adds, "See these blades? With this one, you can open up many cars . . . and with this little one, the whole dashboard comes apart." Amelia tells us that she worked with a group of very young kids who stole cars in the city and brought them to a big garage located a few blocks from her house. There, she and a small group of associates took the cars apart and sold the parts to traders from the city of Buenos Aires. "We used to disassemble the cars superfast. The next morning, traders would come and buy from us. It was easy, and the police wouldn't bother us. We would arrange with them beforehand and they would release the area from interference."[7]

THE DEALER

"I was a thief and a dealer [*fui chorro y transa*]," Jorge tells us. He is now in his forties, and he is still reluctant to talk about his recent past. But we took advantage of what his close friends later described as a rare moment of "opening up" to inquire about the risks involved in his criminal activities (that, in his own words, included "almost everything," from car theft to drug dealing). He is now "retired" from crime and has not touched a "joint or a beer . . . for many, many years." The kinds of things he did, and the tragic end of many of his friends, would merit an entire book: "We were a group of eleven kids . . . only three of us are still around. The rest are either in jail or dead—one killed by the police, another one by a storeowner when he was trying to break in, and another one died of AIDS." What concerns us, however, is something more specific: his group's relationship with the police and the National Guard.

"We had an understanding [*un código*]: you always need your neighbor. Many times I escaped from the police by hiding at a neighbor's house. He [the neighbor] knew I'd never ever touch any of his things." Neighbors, he believes, "felt protected. Now, all these *códigos* are broken." And, like most people in the neighborhood, he attributes this change to the new drugs that are now being consumed by the local youth: "It used to be only marijuana and cocaine, and now it's paco, free-base. Now they'd do anything for drugs [*hacen cualquiera*]."

The *antagonistic* relationship that, when robbing, Jorge's group had with the state repressive forces turned into a relationship of *illicit collaboration* when this group engaged in drug dealing. In Jorge's recollections, both the police and the gendarmes are described as equally involved in "the business" (*el negocio*):

> When we first started dealing, in Las Violetas [a nearby poor neighborhood], we had an arrangement with the police. Every weekend they would come to "pick up the envelope" [i.e., to receive their cut]. The cops knew we were selling drugs, but they didn't bother us. They would release the area for us. Now, if you don't pay them every weekend, you are in trouble. You'd end up in jail. Then we moved to another neighborhood. We were selling cocaine, lots of it, there. But there, the gendarmes protected us. The cops worked with a dealer from a different neighborhood. We were with the gendarmes. See . . . it's all about [different] territories, some for the cops, some others for the National Guard.

In two separate interviews, a federal police agent currently working in the area confirmed this. When we asked her about the types of crime that are predominant in Tucci, she confided that "there are all sorts of crimes. The problem is that the [state] police [force] doesn't help; it's involved with the people who commit crimes . . . cops recruit youngsters to rob, to sell drugs [for them] . . . *they are not cops, they are criminals in uniform*" (our emphasis). Police involvement in crime (particularly in drug trafficking) has not gone unnoticed by the courts. In March 2013, five agents from Tucci's police station were indicted, accused of illegal detentions, fabricating reports (falsely accusing neighbors of drug dealing), planting evidence, and (possibly) distributing drugs. The chief of the station was removed when forty bags of marijuana were found inside the precinct, presumably used to plant evidence and/or to distribute in the area. Police-criminal collusion is not simply a matter of "generalized perceptions" among neighbors and/or one or two (possibly disgruntled) cops but a documented and established practice within the force.

This pernicious form of police intervention at the urban margins obeys a logic that has been in place for at least three decades. A former undersecretary of security in the state of Buenos Aires, and a highly perceptive analyst of the state police's (mis)behavior, describes a "perverse relationship between politics, crime and police action" (Sain 2004:87) and the existence of a "dual pact" for the management of crime (Sain 2013). This "dual pact" involves the delegation of security governance by successive government authorities to police chiefs (the police-political power pact). But it also implies that crime, particularly organized crime, is controlled by the police through its involvement in illicit activities (the police-criminal pact).

During the early 1990s, the government of Buenos Aires made an explicit agreement with the state police: in order to attain "respectable levels of public safety" (Sain 2004:85), the government provided the police with a great amount of material and financial resources and an important degree of freedom of action (i.e., unaccountability). The state government also assured the police that it would not intervene in the illegal self-financing activities that had long been developed by the police.[8] This "circuit of illegal self-financing," as Sain calls it, is the product of the participation of key members of the police hierarchy in an "extended network of criminal activities" (2004:86).

Sain's book *El Leviatán Azul* describes in detail how during the past three decades, the police force consolidated two devices of illegal fund-raising (2008:158–59). The first source of illegal funding—known as the "traditional fund" (*caja tradicional*)—came from bribes or fees charged to illegal gambling, prostitution, street vendors, and unauthorized brothels or nightclubs. The second, and more recent, source of illegal funding of police activities—known as the "dirty fund" (*caja sucia*)—came from agents' participation in violent criminality and/or high-profit criminality (drug trafficking, car theft, kidnapping, and human smuggling). As Sain explains in a recent paper (2013):

> Police regulation has been the essential condition for the formation and expansion of the illegal markets of the more diversified and profitable goods and services: that of illegal drugs; that of auto parts and spare parts obtained from dismantling stolen cars; and that of sexual services supplied through the exploitation of persons . . . In the Argentine case, the key player that guaranteed the stability of the [criminal] environment, the secrecy of the business, and the means to consolidate it as an economic enterprise was the police. The support and protection by the "representatives of the law" of criminal groups has been, at this initial level, the principal condition for their development. Certainly, without police protection in Argentina there would be, undoubtedly, drug trafficking, car theft, or human trafficking. But the significant increase of these modalities of crime—and, in particular, the rapid structuring of the illicit markets and economies linked to them—has found in police regulation tremendous momentum.

Illegal practices are thus institutionalized in the police force (Isla and Miguez 2003). Those living at the bottom of the sociosymbolic order are the ones who directly experience the effects of these clandestine connections.[9] Or, as a recent report from the Center for Legal and Social Studies (CELS) puts it, residents of poor neighborhoods in Buenos Aires "live and suffer the consequences of the connections between the local police and various illegal networks, such as those that sell drugs, steal, dismantle, and distribute cars and/or auto parts, and manage brothels" (CELS 2012; see also Dewey 2012).

POLICE BRUTALITY

Police-criminal collusion (including "liberated zones" for criminal activity and police recruitment of youngsters for criminal activity) coexists with police brutality. Arbitrary, unlawful violence is part of the standard operating procedure of the state police in Buenos Aires—especially when poor youth from shantytowns and squatter settlements are involved (CELS 2012; Daroqui 2009).[10] In Arquitecto Tucci, this "penalization of poverty" (Müller 2011:16) has taken the form of an infamous "massacre" in 1987 in which three youngsters from the neighborhood were brutally murdered by the local police, five cases of lethal police violence between 2005 and 2011 (Coordinadora Contra la Represión Policial e Institucional [CORREPI] 2012), and numerous reports on the police's extreme use of physical force. Fernanda's students are keenly aware of this:

> September 23, 2009: My student Yamila tells me that on Saturday, her brother was hanging out with a group of friends. The police were following one of them but made a mistake and caught Yamila's brother, Mario. The cop hit Mario's face with a helmet and hurt him badly. They dragged him and hurt his leg. It looks as if the doctors will have to amputate Mario's leg.

We were also privy to one particular instance of agents' total disregard for basic rights when Agustín, our research collaborator, was accompanying an agitated mother who wanted to hospitalize her addicted son and had gone to the police as her last resort.

Field note excerpt, September 2011: As we were waiting to be attended to, we witnessed the following interaction between a man who rushed into the precinct to denounce a robbery and the police personnel:

MAN: My truck was stolen!!

POLICEMAN 1: Where?

MAN: On the road that leads to the fair [La Salada] . . . I can't remember the name of the street. It's where the local hospital is.

POLICEMAN 1: [The streets are] Andrés Bello and Recondo. Tell me the color and the license plate of your truck.

MAN [*very nervous*]: The plate . . . is . . . I know who the robber was. I saw him. It's Brian, the one who sells drugs. I was coming with my truck full of stuff from the fair and that son of a bitch jumped into the street and pointed his gun at me. I sped up; I was going to run him over.

POLICEMAN 1: You should have run him over! You should have hit him.

MAN: I was going to but he wasn't alone. There were two more men, pointing their guns at me. I know where Brian lives. I'm going to beat the shit out of him. I can tell you where he lives.

POLICEMAN 1: You should have run him over! Nothing would have happened [to you].

POLICEMAN 2: We have units in the area.

In its simplicity, the exchange illustrates one common form of criminality in the neighborhood, the "pirates of the asphalt" who routinely attempt to steal from traders who work at the feria, and one of the ways in which the police seek to address the issue—"just run over" the criminal and "you won't be charged" with a crime.

INCARCERATION

The Janus-faced character of the Argentine state is well known. The state, as described above, partakes in crime, and it is also selectively active in its repression. While, according to Sain (2009:143), "police tutelage" (i.e., protection and monitoring) is crucial to understanding the territorial expansion of the market of illicit drugs,[11] rates of incarceration in federal prisons have grown almost 400 percent in the past twenty years, fed, to a great extent, by the imprisonment of petty drug dealers and consumers (CELS 2009). As a result, the prison is now a regular presence in the lives of Arquitecto Tucci residents, many of which have relatives behind bars or recently released.

> Little daughter of mine, Estrellita, I'm sorry for everything that is happening. I promise you that it will never happen again. When I get out of here, we are going to be together always and never again will you have to go through this. You know that I love you and your dad too. When I am with you both, we won't suffer anymore. In two or three months I'll be back so you can visit me. Don't be sad. Be a good girl, listen to Grandma, and do your schoolwork.

Estrella (eleven years old) arrived late to school today. We never saw her so happy. "I went to see my mom," she says, excited. And she shows us the letter that her mom, Susana, wrote her. Susana is serving a five-year prison sentence for drug trafficking. The prison is an hour and a half from where Estrella lives now with her grandmother. Her father and her granddad are also in prison for trafficking. "I took her sugar, cigarettes, yerba, and *milanesas*. My grandma took me to see her," Estrella tells us. Susana was transferred to a closer prison so that her family (her mother and her four children) could visit her during five days. It had been three years since the last time Estrella saw her. "She is okay," she tells us. "She says that it's okay, and I see that she is fatter." While she shares this, Estrella caresses and shows us her new ring and her new bracelet: "My mom made them for me. She made them in the jail and today she gave them to me." She also received a necklace with a medallion that says "Susana" on one side and "I love you" on the other.

Fernanda met Susana before she was arrested. She used to live in a very precarious house of sheet metal with a dirt floor. When Susana had her youngest daughter by Caesarean section, in the local school they organized a collection to help her, and they also helped her so that she obtained a subsidy for her family. Her house didn't have a kitchen and she couldn't even heat milk for her children. Due to her extreme poverty, it's difficult to imagine that she was anything more than a small-time and recently initiated drug pusher (*transa*).

Estrella arrives late every day of the week. It is understandable; her time with her mother is much more important than school. "Today I took her cold cuts [*fiambre*], and cigarettes . . . We ate little sandwiches together, sitting at some little tables that they have in jail. They made me take off my ring, my bracelet, and my necklace to enter. There are police who check us all over, everything. They made me take off my clothes." Estrella tells us that her brother didn't want to go to the prison with her today; he has been crying all day. "He loves my mom a lot. He doesn't want them to take her far away."

Estrella is not an isolated case. A third of Fernanda's students in 2011 had a close relative in prison. According to the data provided by CELS, in Buenos Aires, the incarceration rate rose from 71 for every 100,000 inhabitants in 1990 to 198 per 100,000 in 2010. Almost 70 percent of the 30,000 people who suffer inhumane conditions in the prisons of Buenos Aires have not received a sentence; 30 percent of them will be declared innocent when their cases conclude, according to data from the government itself. Seventy-eight percent of the prison population in Buenos Aires Province is between eighteen and forty-four years of age (96 percent are men) and they come from the most disadvantaged sectors: 7 percent never attended an educational institution, 23 percent did not finish elementary school, 53 percent finished elementary school, 13 percent dropped out of high school. At the moment of arrest, more than half did not have employment.

These figures, forceful as they are, tell us little about something that Estrella's story points to and about which many of the testimonies of Fernanda's students alerted us: the concrete effects of increasing incarceration or, more specifically, the ways in which the prison socializes not only those who are housed there but also their family members, partners, sons, and daughters. We know little about the ways in which the prison system, today a constant presence in the neighborhoods of relegation that have multiplied in Buenos Aires Province over the last three decades, affects the daily life of the poor. One of these effects became obvious to us during our fieldwork: with their fathers or mothers (or both) behind bars (85 percent of women incarcerated at the federal level have children; three, on average, according to a recent study by CELS [2012]), boys and girls from the most disadvantaged sectors are forced to take on adult roles (feed their parents, restrain the emotions of their little siblings, etc.) when they have hardly reached adolescence.

Fernanda cannot hide her tears from reading the letter from Estrella's mother. Her students are surprised. Never before had they seen her cry. While she tries to recompose herself and resume class (the topic today is fractions), a student quietly approaches her desk. Noelia, one of her students, hands her a piece of paper, carefully folded. It is a letter from her father, who has been in jail for the past four years. Like Susana's, Pedro's letter speaks of a future safe from suffering and full of love "when I leave this ugly place." Every day, Noelia brings this letter to school, kept safe in her folder.

Any attempt to understand the daily violence in the neighborhood cannot fail to take into account a crucial fact: today, unlike two decades ago, the prison has become a constant presence in the daily life of the urban poor.

Wednesday, April 6, 2011 (Fernanda's diary): Jazmín comes up to me at the end of the flag song. She asks me to go "console" her cousin Josiana. I see that she's alone, far from her fellow first graders. "She misses her dad," Jazmín tells me. "He's in jail and she misses him a whole lot."

Our own observations (and dozens of local newspaper accounts) attest to the fact that the local police publicly and aggressively go after some dealers and thieves. However, as illustrated by the testimonies above (and many more that reasons of space prevent us from presenting), and by accounts from other poverty enclaves throughout Latin America (notably, in Rio de Janeiro's favelas [Gay 2005; Arias 2006; Perlman 2010]), the local police also protect some dealers and thieves, thus becoming an integral part of the crime they (say they) seek to combat. "It is easy to make a deal with the police . . . they come to you for their commission. Every night, you need to give them five or six hundred pesos and they leave you alone," two women involved in petty drug dealing told us. Furthermore, the police are key participants in the black market of guns and bullets. Many people we talked to in Arquitecto Tucci know that they can buy a gun or bullets from off-duty members of La Bonaerense.

When pursuing *some* petty neighborhood drug dealers, policemen employed shock and awe tactics, inundating a certain area of the neighborhood with police cars. In cases such as these, sirens, loud orders, and the usual shootouts marked the police's fast and furious presence in the neighborhood. Both parents and one uncle of Malena (one of Fernanda's ten-year-old students) were arrested in such a fashion during the course of our fieldwork.[12]

Law enforcement is not only intermittent and contradictory (in the sense of doing mutually opposed or inconsistent things) but also highly selective. The police chase and incarcerate *some* petty drug dealers or thieves but, as in many other countries in Latin America (Goldstein 2012; Menjívar 2011; Hautzinger 2007), they are slow and hesitant to go after violent partners or sexual predators (for Argentina, see Amnistía Internacional 2008). We repeatedly heard stories about domestic violence in which the police were nowhere to be found. A social worker at the local school puts it this way, "If a woman goes to the precinct to accuse her husband, the cops just laugh at her." And the two police agents at the office of gender violence at the local precinct tell us that, "these days, women are using *the excuse* of violence to get rid of their husbands," implying that domestic assault is not a real pressing issue (our emphasis). As said before, police agents are also slow in reacting to sexual violence and/or complicit with it.[13]

In Arquitecto Tucci, law enforcement is fast *and* sluggish, watchful *and* neglectful, depending on the kind of wrongdoing and the parties involved. As a result, residents suffer all sorts of victimization but are unwilling to call on the police because they intuitively know that agents will not act on their claims, or they suspect that they are either the perpetrators of crime or in close association with criminals. Take the case of local drug dealers (publicly known as *transas*): Neighbors are fearful of going to the local precinct and denouncing their operations because they think that *transas* will learn about their reports (from the cops) and will retaliate against them. At a local meeting we attended, neighbors said this quite explicitly: "Everybody knows where the dealers live, and everybody knows that the police are in cahoots with them . . . and we are afraid that if we report the dealers, we'll suffer the consequences." Drawing on the language we used before to describe the form that violence takes in the neighborhood, we could say that they are afraid of the possible "concatenation of victimization."[14]

Unsurprisingly then, one common theme defines the local point of view on the subject of police intervention. Residents perceive the neighborhood as a "liberated zone": an area where perpetrators of all sorts of illicit activities can do as they please (or, as one neighbor put it at a community meeting devoted to discussing issues of safety and crime, as a place where "anything goes"). The outcome of this intermittent and contradictory police intervention is thus a variation of what David Kirk and Andrew Papachristos call "legal cynicism"—the shared belief that law enforcement agents are "illegitimate, unresponsive, and ill equipped to ensure public safety" (2011:1191). But, in Arquitecto Tucci, different from the US ghetto or poor barrio, legal cynicism emerges not simply out of the perceived unavailability or bias of law enforcement agents but also out of the complicity between cops and criminals. Local violence has a clear political underpinning because of the irregular involvements of state authorities in the neighborhood that not only "liberate the zone" to alternative and violent modes of law and order but that also often promote and perpetuate violent crime and interpersonal violence.

In "On Transformations of Aggressiveness," Elias writes that, in the Middle Ages, "[r]obbing, fighting, hunting men and animals—all this formed part and parcel of everyday life" (1978:237). Only gradually, as a "central power strong enough to compel restraint" begins to grow, do people feel constrained to "live in peace with one another." Relative restraint and "consideration of people for one another" increase in everyday life, and "not just anyone who chances to be strong can enjoy the pleasure of physical aggression" (ibid. 238). In other words, for Elias (1994; 1978), the relatively peaceful collective life of large masses of people in a given territory is, in good part, based on the actions of a state that consistently pacifies the social spaces in which people interact. What we have shown is the exact opposite of the "civilizing process" that Elias describes. The intermittent, contradictory, and selective ways in which law enforcement works at the urban margins reinforces the violence that regularly puts the poor in harm's way.

In a now classic piece, political scientist Guillermo O'Donnell offers a complement to Elias's theory of the civilizing process that serves to further clarify the current predicament of Argentine marginalized neighborhoods. In "On the State, Democratization and Some Conceptual Problems," O'Donnell describes the existence of "neofeudalized regions" where "the obliteration of legality deprives the regional power circuits, including those state agencies, of the public, lawful dimension without which the national state and the order it supports vanish" (1993:1359). In what he famously called "brown areas," state organizations become part of a privatized circuit of power, the public dimension of the state evaporates, and, as a consequence, we have a "democracy of low-intensity citizenship" (ibid. 1361). The less-advantaged populations, of the kind that inhabit our field site, are usually the ones who are the most affected by this destruction of the rule of law:

> [P]easants, slum dwellers, Indians, women, etc. often are unable to receive fair treatment in the courts, or to obtain from state agencies services to which they are entitled, or to be safe from political violence, etc. . . . [I]n many brown areas the democratic, participatory rights of polyarchy are respected. But the liberal component of democracy is systematically violated. A situation in which one can vote freely and have one's vote counted fairly, but cannot expect proper treatment from the police or the courts, puts in serious question the liberal component of that democracy and severely curtails citizenship. (ibid.)

The relegated urban area where we conducted our fieldwork is not exactly a "brown area," where state presence is "very low or nil," but something much more complex and empirically more challenging. The issue at stake is not state absence, collapse, or weakness but of police-criminal "collusion" of the kind described by Desmond Arias in Rio de Janeiro's favelas—an "active political constellation" that promotes violence (2006). In other words, the scenario described above is not one of "state abandonment" but of connections between state actors and perpetrators of violence—an "engagement" that erodes the rule of law, institutes "a separate, localized, order" (ibid. 324), and reproduces high levels of interpersonal violence.

The violence that suffuses the lives of poor people in Tucci lacks the redemptive properties that Franz Fanon, to use a classic example, attributes to the violence of the subaltern. The violence under examination here is neither a "cleansing force" that "frees the native from his inferiority complex and from his despair and inaction" (Fanon 1990:74) nor an energy that makes the poor "fearless" or restores their "self-respect" (for a full discussion, see Bernstein 2013). Furthermore, the street violence placed under the ethnographic microscope here is not the subaltern violence that, oftentimes dissected by historians and social scientists, is directed against the state, the powerful, or its symbols (Davis 1973; Darnton 2006; Thompson 1994; Scott 1985; Steinberg 1999).

Although this violence is not used by the oppressed or the excluded as a weapon to reconfigure structures of domination or as a strategy to assert and/or celebrate popular power, *it does have a political character*. In this chapter, we showed that this violence among the poor is political because it is deeply entangled with the intermittent, selective, and contradictory form in which the state intervenes in this neighborhood of relegation through its police force. In chapter 4, we will show that violence is also political in that (a) it has the potential to give birth to collective action that targets the state while simultaneously signaling it as the main actor responsible for the skyrocketing physical aggression in the area, and (b) it provokes paradoxical forms of informal social control as residents rely on state agents who are themselves enmeshed in the production of this violence.

As mentioned above, neighbors do occasionally come together to talk about crime, drugs, and public safety, and to discuss what to do about them. In March 2013, a group of twenty or so residents met immediately after the murder of an old-time resident and organized a rally to protest "rising violence and drug dealing," and "police complicity." The meeting and the rally point to the fact that interpersonal violence is political not only because the state is implicated in its production but also because it can engender a type of collective action that addresses the state. But collective action is just one of the possible responses to widespread risk and violence. There are others ways of dealing and coping that also merit ethnographic attention. Residents sometimes resort to the police to discipline and punish their loved ones. Other times, they unleash further violence in their attempts to pacify their households. In chapter 4, we will dissect these different practices and scrutinize their ethical and political dimensions.

CHAPTER 4

ETHICS AND POLITICS AMID VIOLENCE

After the unexpected death of their daughter Amy, Roger and Ginny moved to her house and began a new life as grandparents, helping their son-in-law care for three very young children. A few years later, Roger Rosenblatt wrote a memoir, *Making Toast*, where he vividly and quite movingly describes his thoughts and feelings after his daughter's untimely death and the new life that, after such devastating loss, they began with their grandchildren. "I come up very early in the morning, set the table for the children, and then when they come down make toast for those who want it. Sometimes cinnamon toast, sometimes regular toast," Rosenblatt told NPR's Melissa Block. "The only reason I wanted *Making Toast* as the title is that it is a simple gesture of moving on. Every morning there's the bread and you make the toast and you start the day. And so, even unconsciously, it became a symbol of how to live our life."

The daily routine of making toast is, in Rosenblatt's view, a "simple gesture" of moving on, to keep on living amid (and while coping with) deep psychological pain. While routines arguably help ground all of human life, as Rosenblatt's story alludes to, these routines may take on a particular resonance under specific sets of circumstances, such as the loss of a loved one. Regular, ordinary practices such as "making toast"—whether carried over from the past or created in the present—provide order and predictability (you make toast *every morning*) and tie people together through acts of care (you make toast *for the children*) in times of instability and uncertainty. In this chapter, we examine the routines, akin to "making toast," that residents of Tucci deploy to deal with surrounding danger.

People not only rely on routines to deal and cope with daily exposure to violence but other practices, less routinized yet equally prevalent and relevant, are used to navigate such contexts. "I know how to defend myself," fifty-two-year-old Sonia said during a long interview at the local community center. "I learned how to kill since I was a little kid. My grandfather taught me; he made me practice with an apple, splitting it with my little hands." In this chapter we show that, along with "making toast," people living in high-risk environments cope with violence by "splitting apples." When a grandfather teaches his granddaughter how to kill a man by having her practice on a fruit, or when, as we oftentimes heard during fieldwork, a mother chains her daughter to her bed so that the teenage daughter cannot feed her drug addiction, we see that residents respond to violence not only with routine acts but also with nonroutine, violent practices.

In this chapter, the central starting point is this ordering and relational character of routines and practices that are akin to making toast and splitting apples. We investigate the different ways—some that are mundane and/or routine, others that are not; some that involve the perpetration of physical damage, others that do not—that Tucci residents draw on in order to cope with (and respond to) the constant, but also unpredictable, danger that besieges them and their loved ones. Drawing on the work of Das (2012) and Lambek (2010), we argue that these routine and nonroutine practices, *including* those that involve the deployment of violence, can be understood as the expression of "ordinary ethics," or the "small disciplines that ordinary people perform in their everyday life to hold life as the natural expression of ethics" (Das 2012:139). Violence, as many social science accounts attest (Anderson 1999; Bourgois 2003; Das 1990; Garbarino 1993), shatters and unravels routine daily existence. But a plethora of "small acts [that] allow life to be knitted pair by pair" (Das 2012:139) also exists. The ethical (here understood as a sense of duty of what is the correct thing to be done, i.e., a moral striving [Lambek 2010]) lies precisely there, and the aim of this chapter is to locate, unearth, and dissect these "raveling" practices, particularly expressions of care amid a violence that corrodes community life.[1]

Adopting neither a romantic nor a sanitized approach to the actions of those living in highly dangerous, destitute neighborhoods (Contreras 2012; Gowan 2010; Wacquant 2002), we engage with the difficult question of what it means when care practices end up (re)producing significant forms of violence, such as when parents use harsh physical force to discipline their children or when neighbors physically punish adolescents to "teach them a lesson." We argue that these acts of sometimes extreme violence should be understood and explained with an eye toward the challenges that parents, and especially mothers, face in trying to keep their children safe—and often just alive—under extremely precarious conditions (see Jones 2009).

Residents of communities plagued by violence are acutely aware of the hazards that chronic exposure to interpersonal physical harm poses, and they express a deep desire to protect their loved ones and make active efforts to do so despite the many constraints they face (Zubillaga et al. forthcoming; Penglase 2010). However, while sociological and journalistic accounts of life in dangerous communities point to some of the more spectacular ways in which people respond to danger, such as direct retaliation (Kotlowitz 1991; Bourgois 1995;

Anderson 1999; Alarcón 2003, 2009; LeBlanc 2004; Venkatesh 2008; Jones 2009; Harding 2010; Gay 2005), collective organizing (Hume 2009), and lynching and/or vigilantism (Snodgrass Godoy 2002; Goldstein 2012; Ayala and Derpic 2013), we still know little about the less public and often, though not always, mundane practices and routines that residents under siege devise to prevent violence and protect their loved ones.

We draw attention here to the multiple practices in which residents in Arquitecto Tucci engage in order to regain a sense of control among the murders, shootings, robberies, and sexual attacks that unsettle and disrupt daily life. Some of these practices take the consistent form of a "routine," or what the *Oxford English Dictionary* describes as "a regular course of procedure; a more or less mechanical or unvarying performance of certain acts or duties." Routines, many a sociological study shows, have an ordering effect. They orient and stimulate action, "shape attention and structure thinking" (Heimer 2001:50; see also Lazaric 2000; Eden 2004), and, importantly, in the wake of disruptive circumstances, such as in the aftermath of disasters (e.g., Noveck 2012), comfort and soothe. Much like making toast did for Rosenblatt, we found that minute acts, like establishing and following nightly curfews or walking together to the bus stop at dawn, helped to provide an important antidote to counteract the many unknowns that residents of Arquitecto Tucci face on a daily basis.

The same residents who organized group trips to the bus stop, or introduced schedules to their families, were also the same residents who taught their sons and daughters how to fight, or, if they feared for their safety, tied up their sons and daughters to prevent them from doing drugs and/or beat them in the name of protecting them from further harm. We draw on our data to suggest that both making toast and splitting apples exist in the same continuum of care—though violence, most typically, arises as a "last resort tool of care."

By focusing on daily, ordinary routines, in this chapter we draw attention not only to activities that occur within households but to the many occasions in which neighbors and friends band together in care practices and routines in an attempt to mitigate exposure to violence. In other words, despite a generalized climate of fear that has paralyzing and isolating effects (Rotker 2002; Caldeira 2000), residents do respond, sometimes individually, other times in coordination with others, to violence. Many of these seemingly minute acts, we argue, reveal an *ethics of care*—a sense of duty that becomes articulated through the specific ways that some look after the most vulnerable.

By examining social practices akin to Rosenblatt's making toast, we draw attention to the additional (and often unnoticed) labor that mainly women and mothers do to protect loved ones, in this case, from the constant threat of muggings, sexual assault, burglaries, and even death—or what Sinikka Elliot and Elyshia Aseltine have termed "protective carework" (2013).[2]

Residents in Arquitecto Tucci respond to interpersonal violence in a variety of ways. A basic catalog of ways of coping should include: (a) *individualized nonviolent responses*, as when residents seclude themselves inside their homes, reinforce the supervision of their children, bolster their own precautions when venturing into public space, fortify their homes, and (occasionally) report incidents to the police; (b) *individualized violent responses*, as when residents forcibly confine their children when they perceive them as "getting in trouble" or beat (actual or potential) perpetrators of violence (including their own children) and/or those who are thought to be "bad influences"; (c) *collective violent responses*, as when residents attack the homes of rapists and beat perpetrators or physically punish a thief; and (d) *collective nonviolent responses*, as when residents come together in meetings and public rallies to protest police inaction (and complicity with crime) and demand state protection, or when they organize a public shaming of known drug dealers. These are analytical distinctions that get blurred in daily practice. The same people who seclude their families to protect themselves and their loved ones from street violence may also rely on physical constraint or violence to keep children from "falling in with the wrong crowd" (*las malas compañías*, as they put it).

This chapter begins with a description of the nonviolent practices and routines that neighbors develop in the midst of violence. We then turn to more enigmatic and paradoxical practices that involve the threat and/or actual use of violence and the involvement of the arm of the state, which most in the neighborhood see as deeply implicated in the production of violence. In both forms of action, we unearth an ethics of care at work. We end the chapter with an examination of a peaceful form of collective action that is slowly emerging in the neighborhood to tackle the issue of public safety and with a (hopeful) speculation regarding the character of this incipient social movement.

CARE PRACTICES AND ROUTINES

During the course of fieldwork, residents told us repeatedly that "there's nothing you can do" about the widespread violence in their community. Laura (fifty-one), a long-term resident, told us: "People here are scared if you do something; they [the perpetrators] might get you and hit you or your family. They may retaliate." Similarly, Verónica (forty-four) told us: "People do not report it to the police because they are scared." And during a community meeting we attended, most residents seemed to agree that fear has a demobilizing impact: "There are a lot of people who are angry about all this insecurity, but they are afraid to come to the meetings . . . they don't want to report anything because they are afraid they won't be able to go back to their homes." Fear, residents agreed, "paralyzes us all." Despite their expressions of fear, impotence, and "futility" (Bandura 1982), our ethnographic fieldwork revealed a multitude of ways in which the residents of Arquitecto Tucci attempt to mitigate exposure to violence for themselves and loved ones: a welcome reminder of the distance between what people say and what they do (see Jerolmack and Khan 2014).

One of the most common responses to violence in Arquitecto Tucci is the fortification of homes. Like middle-class families across the Americas (Caldeira 2000; Svampa 2001), residents of Arquitecto Tucci build walls to separate their homes from the streets and alleyways, install stronger doors ("so they can't kick it down and break in"), and add padlocks to their windows. Not only do these investments make residents feel safer when they are at home but they also make them feel more comfortable in venturing away, which provides peace of mind that the people, and the things they leave behind, will remain safe. The following exchange between Verónica and Marta, who are in their mid-forties and have adolescent children, illustrates this point:

VERÓNICA: This door is not strong enough. They can kick it down . . . but she has good doors, in the front and in the back.

MARTA: Yes, I have no problems. I can lock the doors and put padlocks on the windows. They are very strong. But she can't leave the house. They can break in and take all her stuff away.

Not surprisingly, one common way that residents attempt to avoid violence is through regular seclusion in the homes that they have fortified from the outside world. "I stay in my room, watch TV, and don't get involved with anybody," explains one resident. "Right after dinner, we all get inside, and we padlock our door . . . When the street market [La Salada] is open, there are many robberies, and there's always some crazy kid with a gun, and they might shoot at each other, and a stray bullet might hit my kids . . . So, we stay inside. We try to keep the same schedule every day," explains another resident.

The keeping of regular timetables ("We keep the same schedule every day"; "By 5:00 p.m., everybody should be inside . . . we have dinner at 8:00 p.m."), and especially curfews, emerges as a particularly important tool for the residents of Arquitecto Tucci in dealing with a hostile environment. Following a schedule provides consistency and a sense of control in what is a fundamentally unpredictable environment—an anchor in the midst of a maelstrom of violence. A curfew, for instance, creates a boundary between what is a "safe" and "unsafe" time for residents to occupy public space. As long as residents return home by the self-defined point at which danger becomes too widespread and unpredictable to risk (in their minds), they can feel relatively "safe."

Sheltering is often coupled with extra supervision of children, with parents (mainly mothers) keeping close tabs on where and with whom their sons and daughters spend their time. Mothers in the neighborhood have an intuitive understanding of early psychiatric research: "[S]trict parental supervision and regulation of children's peer group activities outside the home reduces the risk of delinquency for children reared in a high-risk environment" (Rutter 1987:326). Norma (thirty-four), explains, "I take care of my kids by talking to them, by checking with whom they get together, by not letting them out after certain hours." Similarly, Marta (forty) says, "You have to check on their *compañías* [the company they keep] all the time."

Fearing for their safety in public spaces—"You can't go to work in peace. I'm always looking around to see if someone is following me, always watching my back," explains one resident—adult neighbors take a number of precautions when venturing outside their homes. For example, residents young and old typically avoid traveling alone, especially at night. "I don't walk around . . . I always take a car service when it gets dark," explains Zulma (forty-one). "I always make sure someone waits for me at the bus stop," says another resident. Like adults, youngsters tend to travel together, operating under the belief that there is safety in numbers: the neighborhood, they tell us, is "dangerous . . . it got ugly in the last few years." In a conversation at the local high school, one student (sixteen) explains: "We go to parties with our friends, in a pack . . . always. You need a big group to go out, and it's better if someone in the group is really a badass, so that . . . you know . . . nothing bad happens to you. If you go out in a small group, or worse, by yourself . . . the *chorros* [thieves] would grab you and steal your stuff, your sneakers."

Thus, although community violence does breed isolation, we also see that it generates certain routines (i.e., regular courses of action) that require connectivity within the household (as when there's a need to coordinate who stays and who leaves, and who goes with whom to the bus stop) and among friends and acquaintances (as when youngsters organize their outings; for a similar argument in Monterrey's [Mexico] poor neighborhoods, see Villarreal forthcoming).

The protective weapons of those living in harm's way, to paraphrase and adapt James Scott (1985), are similar, irrespective of the nature of the threat (be it the theft of sneakers or sexual assault). "I try to be with them," says Gloria (thirty-eight) about her children, "close to them, to avoid something bad happening to them. I don't want them to be far from me . . . Anything can happen to them; these days there are many daring men [*atrevidos*]. There are men who abuse young girls. I try to get them to stay inside, to not leave the house." Similarly, María (forty-one) states: "You have to be with them all the time. They [María's children] have to call me often if they are outside."

Residents are responsible for bearing the brunt of the labor involved in keeping loved ones and themselves safe (embedded in care practices and routines, as we have shown here). This points to the larger structural context that shapes Arquitecto Tucci and other marginalized neighborhoods across the Americas—the state, as we examined in chapter 3, is typically negligent in regards to protecting the poor from violence, if not complicit in this violence.

Above we have shown that residents of Arquitecto Tucci (despite their frequent claims otherwise) engage in a variety of practices—many of these taking the regular form that characterizes routines—to protect themselves and their loved ones. Residents seclude themselves inside their homes, strengthen the supervision of their children, bolster their own precautions when venturing into public space (traveling in groups, accompanying each other to take the bus, etc.), monitor the movements of friends and/or acquaintances, fortify their homes and/or take turns guarding the home, and (occasionally) report incidents to the police. These practices expose an *ethics of care*—or, to borrow the words of Hayder Al-Mohammad and Daniela Peluso (2012), "an ethics of the rough ground." Practices and routines provide order amid chaos, and help residents establish normalcy in their lives.

The fact that women were more likely to be recorded or to report engagement in, and to be in charge of, these practices and routines is not an artifact of our research design but is further evidence of the "gendered division of labor," in which women, rather than men, are tasked with caring for others' needs, including those of children, the elderly, and the disabled (Thistle 2006). In Arquitecto Tucci, where physical injury, sexual assault, and death looms large, keeping loved ones out of harm's way, not surprisingly, emerges as one of the most essential undertakings for the (mainly) women tasked with exerting "care." In Arquitecto Tucci, it is not only that women are tasked with responsibility for the care and keeping of their families, which is increasingly common in poor neighborhoods in Latin America (Neumann 2013), but they are also the only eligible adults available in the household to adopt these responsibilities.

VIOLENCE, POLICE, AND PRISON AS PROTECTIVE CAREWORK

The protective and coping practices and routines described above find parallels in poor and violent communities throughout the Americas (Goldstein 1998, 2003; Hautzinger 2007; Penglase 2010; Jones 2009; Menjívar 2011). More enigmatic, and much less explored in the literature, is the teaching and use of physical force in the name of the prevention of (and protection from) violence. As hinted at in the stories presented in chapter 2, in Arquitecto Tucci, adults teach children how to use violence to protect themselves; forcibly (and sometimes brutally) confine children perceived as "getting in trouble"; and beat (actual or potential) perpetrators of violence (including their own children) and/or those who are thought to be "bad influences." In this section we examine these practices and consider how they emerge as "last resort" tools of "care."

One main way that parents and other adults try to extend protection to children is through teaching them how to utilize violence, typically for use in self-defense. The following story vividly illustrates this point.

Sonia (fifty-two) tells us that she has mastered "killing techniques since she was very young" and later adds, "they trained me to kill." Sonia wasn't speaking metaphorically. "My grandpa trained me . . . my older brother was a pervert, a degenerate, and I am the youngest of my sisters."

"Sonia," my grandpa said to me, "one day your brother is going to come to hurt you, and when that happens, it's either you or him. You can't give in." Like that my grandpa told me. And he trained me to kill, so that my brother couldn't rape me . . . If my brother someday came to rape me, I wasn't going to be able to punch him, choke him, nothing, because he was bigger than me. But my grandpa taught me that the only way to defend myself that I had was to dig my nails here, in the bone that you guys have in the throat [the Adam's apple] and turn my hand as hard as I can until I tear it out. That kills you."

Sonia took an apple from the kitchen and placed her thumbs on the bottom and the rest on the top of the fruit. "I was five, six, no more than seven years old," she says, "and my grandpa made me grab an apple like this and I had to dig my fingernails into it. Once I dug in my nails, I had to twist my hands until I was able to separate it into two halves. When he told me that, I set myself to practicing until I could break the apple." The apple made a "tac" sound as Sonia split it into two.

Sonia's entire life has been shaped by violence. She shares: "My first memory is that my old man wanted to smash my mother's head with a metal tank. I was three years old. My sister took me in her arms, crying out for help, so that someone would help my mom." She also remembers brutal fights between her brothers: "When my brothers fought, in my house, it was to kill or die."

Sonia's grandfather taught Sonia to utilize violence in an effort to help protect her from the real and looming threats to her well-being, and absent other viable recourses for increasing her safety.[3] In this way, and along the line proposed earlier, the teaching of violence can be thought of as embodying an "ethics of care," or in other words, as a form of "protective carework." We would be remiss not to note, however, that Sonia's use of this "learned" violence diverged from self-protection into the victimization of others. The efforts of parents and loved ones to keep their children safe, can, we found, end up contributing to the chronic violence that plagues the community (and from which they have attempted to make their family immune).

More difficult to understand than why parents and other adults sometimes teach young ones how to use violence in the interest of fostering the latter's ability to protect themselves is the frequent use of physical force utilized against sons and daughters in the name of keeping children safe. Physical aggression is used by parents to discipline sons and daughters and to prevent potential violence, and by neighbors to "educate" youngsters who are deemed problematic. Fists, kicks, sticks, and chains are deployed to make children stay away from *malas compañías* (friends deemed bad influences) or, if they "already fell," to try to control their addiction to drugs or alcohol and the violent behavior that ensues. Refrains such as "Next time I see you with a joint, I'll break your fingers"; "He came home so drugged up, I punched him in the face until blood came out of my fingers"; and "I chained her to the bed so that she couldn't go out and smoke" were disturbingly common throughout our fieldwork.

Recall Ana's beating of Leonardo, described in chapter 2 ("I hit him with the broom. I hit him everywhere, arms, legs . . . I lost it . . . I swear to you, I lost it, I didn't want to stop beating him until I could see blood coming out"). While particular in its details, the following vignette further illustrates the context-dependent deployment of violence by adults (and mainly mothers) against their sons and daughters.

Daniel (twenty) "has been smoking pot since he was four-teen," his mother Fabiana (forty-two) tells us, "but it was okay, nothing terrible happened to him, until paco appeared . . . I've seen him drugged with it, and it's terrible." Last Christmas, Fabiana lost track of him for more days than usual (he tends to disappear from home for a couple days, only to come back, his clothes in rags, dirty, and exhausted from long days and nights of smoking paco). In desperation, Fabiana went looking for him. "I searched for him everywhere . . . I ended up in an abandoned house, one of those houses the kids use to store and consume drugs . . . It was night, pitch-black, and I recognized the sound of his laughter. Two kids there wanted to stop me, but I told them to let me in or I'd call the cops. I started dialing 911 and they let me in. I got ahold of Daniel and beat the shit out of him. He doesn't remember I punched him; he doesn't remember where he was. He doesn't remember anything." After that episode, Fabiana tried to monitor Daniel's movements more closely—"my acquaintances send me text messages when they see him; they tell me if he is consuming or not."

As the story of Ana and Leonardo before, this one also involves the recollection of a mother's use of violence against a teenage/young adult son who frequently used freebase cocaine (paco). In both cases, the latter disappeared for days or weeks at a time, and when they returned home, they disrupted the household through their own threat or use of violence and/or by engaging in theft of the households' valuable (and scarce) resources. Although we cannot access exactly what made Fabiana and Ana engage in these acts of violence against their sons in the moment (and suspect that the driving motivations behind these acts are complex, multiple, and likely change throughout the course of committing violence), neither do we think that these acts can be understood as pure cruelty, that is, the intentional imposition of physical pain with the intention of causing anguish or fear (Shklar 1985).

Hours of listening to mothers recount brutal acts against their children reveal not only the mechanics of violence (the form of the punch, the marks left on the victim's body), but also, and more important, the frustration and impotence that mothers experience in the course of attempting to protect their children, especially when they feel that these efforts are being actively thwarted by their children's or other loved ones' own actions. This frustration is illustrated in Alicia's (fifty-five) recounting of her use of violence against Ezequiel (seventeen), a friend of her son Victor (twenty-seven): "When Ezequiel came back to the house," recalls Alicia, "he was about to smoke another pipe [of paco]. I struck him across his face. 'Son of a bitch,' I told him, 'Don't you see that you are making your mother suffer? She is very worried about you. And don't you even think about hurting her, because I'll strike you harder next time.'" According to Alicia, Ezequiel needs to "respect" his mother, a respect that Ezequiel's mother needs, Alicia believes, to earn for herself—with the use violence if necessary: "I have been a thief [*pirata del asfalto*], I've done drugs, I've carried weapons . . . And yet, my kids always respected me. And when they didn't, I made myself respected . . . my son, Victor, stills has the marks of the chain I used to hit him on the head."

Alicia repeatedly hit her son on the head with a chain, and she also used that chain to tie him to the bed: "When Victor was on drugs, he didn't obey me. He used to escape from our house all the time. I chained him so that he wouldn't leave his room. I cried for him so many times. I told him that I didn't enjoy hitting him but that I did it because he was on drugs." All this violence, however, did not stop Victor's addiction; prison time did. As Alicia recalls, he "finally quit using drugs when he went to jail for a robbery he did not commit." As with the majority of inmates that are currently doing time in Buenos Aires prisons, Victor never had a firm judicial sentence—that is, he was imprisoned under a pretrial detention—and was released after three years and eight months in a state prison. That "time," Alicia is convinced, did him well. He is now "cured."

If we keep listening—as we did during the many difficult hours of ethnographic interviewing—mixed in with this palpable, overwhelming frustration and felt loss of control, another possible motivation for these mothers' use of violence emerges: the mothers' belief that violence was the only means remaining to prevent an even less desirable outcome than the marks they sometimes put on their children's bodies, or than the fear and trauma they may have inspired in their children through their violent acts. Their violence, as they saw it, was a last-ditch effort to interrupt addiction, keep their children away from bad influences who might endanger them, keep them out of prison, and/or end the cycle of young death in the community. Violence is thus seen as an expression of care, as a rightful way of looking after others. For many a mother of an addicted son or daughter, violence is constructed not as a practice they want to engage in but rather as the only option for keeping their offspring out of further harm's way ("I can't do anything else other than beat him").

Our ethnographic work reveals that mothers are both correct in their assessments of their sons' and daughters' level of danger (especially for those who "fall"), and in their assessments of how few options exist for helping children to recover from drug use or to escape a drug-dealing clique. When we understand that mothers in this community have few options for saving a child from impending danger, it becomes possible to see why, in very specific and extreme circumstances, violence can become understood—from the view of the perpetrator—as a "last resort tool of care." Thus, through careful scrutiny of the context in which mothers aim to raise their children, it becomes possible to understand and explain how and why violence emerges as a tool of care, and how that practice may stick in the larger context of what it means to be a "good mother" in Arquitecto Tucci.

One last vignette from our field notes further illustrates the difficult choices that mothers face, as well as how violence emerges as one possible (and even understandable) response to those choices. This is Claudia (forty-two), talking about her son Rubén (seventeen).

> Rubén had disappeared for a few days. We couldn't find him anywhere. We looked everywhere. One day we got a text message saying that he was in the [nearby] squatter settlement. He was with this "junta" [bad company], taking drugs. I went with my husband to pick him up. When we returned home, I took him to the bathtub; he was all dirty. And I beat the shit out of him. I used a stick, and I smashed it in his back—I swear I am not a bad mother. But I don't know what else to do. The next day, we went to the drug rehab center [to try to intern him], to see what we could do. And he told the therapist there that I had beaten him. But he didn't tell her that we had to pay $450 to the dealers. He owed that much to the dealers, and if he didn't pay, they would kill him.

While Claudia may have acted out of anger and frustration, her actions are also a response to feeling as if no other choices existed to protect her son.

Above, we have already discussed the wariness with which most residents of Arquitecto Tucci approach the police for aid, though they sometimes do—in what typically involves a desperate attempt to save sons and daughters from the dangers of drug addiction. Driven by impotence and fear—impotence in the face of the lure of highly addictive substances (such as paco) and fear of having a child either murdered by a drug dealer or gang, or killed from an overdose—parents will, on occasion, summon the punitive arm of the state. For example, Mariela (forty-five), provides this explanation for why she turned her son over to the police: "You can't do anything against drugs . . . I die if he dies . . . you have no idea how I anguish every time I think that he can die because of the drugs." From this perspective, the police force has the same "sociological ambivalence" that the prison system has for many inmates' relatives (Comfort 2008).

The above are not the only cases that exemplify the paradoxical way in which helplessness and fright do not necessarily immobilize residents. Graciela is one of the coordinators of a local soup kitchen that serves adults and children in the neighborhood. During our three-hour conversation, she repeatedly tells us that "here, you have to be careful, you should watch out" (*hay que tener cuidado*). She and Ana, the other soup kitchen coordinator, are talking about the last two murders in the neighborhood—the murder of Carlitos on his sixteenth birthday a few months before and the recent assassination of a policeman. Carlitos was stealing a van from a man who shot him in the back. The policeman resisted when a group of youngsters tried to steal his car. He was shot in front of his family, "his brains splashed all over the place." "If they are going to rob you, you shouldn't fight back," they both agree, "because if you do so, they know it's either you or them."

As they continue talking about the two episodes, a common theme emerges: both, they believe, were fueled by rampant drug consumption. Intuitively articulating what the literature calls the "psychopharmacological" link between drugs and violence, they state that youngsters "get high and they do anything [*hacen cualquiera*]." Then Graciela asserts, "There's nothing you can do against drugs." "What do you do, as mothers, so that your children don't get out of control?" Agustín asks. After a brief moment of silence, Graciela shares with us a story that seems to be representative of many families' experiences in the neighborhood: "One of mine got out of control [*se descontroló*]; he is now in jail [with a six-year sentence for robbery]." Graciela visits him in prison—located in General Alvear, a five-hour bus ride one way—only when she has "some merchandise [food, cigarettes, etc.]" to bring him. "It is not worth the trip if I can't bring him something . . . but I visit him quite often . . . I go by myself. The other day, my other son asked me, 'When is Pirulo coming back? I don't even remember his face.' . . . He is doing well there," Graciela tells us, and then adds, "I want him to be there." Graciela does not want him to be in jail. The "there" refers to that specific prison where, according to her, he is "much safer" than in the previous one where, according to her own account, other inmates "beat the shit out of him" in several disputes over drugs and "almost killed him. . . . This one is a maximum security prison. He is studying there, and he is doing some [drug] rehab. I tried to bring him to rehab several times, but he refused."

Graciela has another younger son who has been in trouble with the law, also for drug consumption and selling. This one, she says, was "lucky." Once cited by the judge, "the judge told him that if he continued like that he was going to go to jail, and that he was not going to do well there. He told him to obey me, and he told me that if I saw something strange, if I saw some suspicious behavior, I could go to him and ask him to put my son behind bars. He gave me the power to do so. I told myself: 'This is my second child; I won't screw it up. If I see that he is into drugs, I'll call the precinct.'" Confident in the beneficial effects of the power bestowed on her by the criminal justice system, Graciela stresses that her second son is now "doing fine. He has a job, he is a scavenger; it's a struggle, but every day he goes out and scavenges." Our long conversation ends with her reflection on the predicament of Liliana, her seventeen-year-old daughter who is sitting by her side: "With her, I don't mess around. I don't allow her to go to any party. She doesn't know what can happen if she goes to a party and there are drugs there, and they make her take drugs."

All these fears are palpable in the way neighbors talk about their neighborhood. They all express concern over the increasing incidence of crime and the need for caution, as well as deep worries about the devastating effects of drugs on the local youth. Out of dread, out of helplessness, mothers either trust or summon the punitive arm of the state (the police and/or the prison system) to control, discipline, or "rehabilitate" the lives of their daughters and sons.[4] Michel Foucault could hardly have come up with a more pernicious example of *governmentality*— that is, a set of subjective (but hardly individual) beliefs and practices through which subjects (in this case, we could even say "willingly") are governed, that is, subordinated to the capillary tentacles of state power—a power that, as we discussed before, often engages in unlawful action and is one of the main forces behind the violence that wrecks the neighborhood.

Thus far we have aimed to redirect focus from the overwhelmingly negative outcomes of violence on individuals and communities explored before to examine the efforts of residents of Arquitecto Tucci to make sense of and navigate a dangerous environment, and their attempts to care for one another amid widespread violence and precarity. Drawing inspiration from Roger Rosenblatt's metaphor of making toast, we focus mainly on the more mundane and less public activities, routines, and care practices that shape the lives of those living at the urban margins, and that are often left out of sociological, anthropological, and journalistic accounts.

Through placing acts at the level of making toast and splitting apples under sociological scrutiny, we begin to see how even small acts, such as setting a family curfew, emerge as important in the lives of those struggling amid what might be called "chronic uncertainty"—a way to establish a sense of normalcy and control in a fundamentally unpredictable environment. We argue that these acts contain what Lambek (2010) and Das (2012) call "ordinary ethics." In their efforts to protect loved ones, residents express an ethics of care. We also noted how these efforts to protect loved ones are profoundly gendered, and fall almost exclusively on women, and especially mothers, in the community.

At a time and a place in which the state (or, more precisely, one of the ways in which the state makes itself present in the neighborhood) constantly violates the rule of law, the presence and operation of an ordinary ethics takes on a special meaning. What Jonathan Shay (1994) writes for another context applies here: the relentless "betrayal of 'what is right,'" makes individual and collective ethical choices even more startling. This, to repeat, is not intended to romanticize these routines and practices but to understand their cultural and political relevance in its specific proper setting.

Despite what they say, residents *do* respond to violence, if not always in ways that would be visible to anyone but a careful observer of how daily life unfolds in this community on the ground. We also show how, in a highly dangerous community such as Arquitecto Tucci, the teaching and use of violence comes to be seen as containing an expression of care. Women and mainly mothers struggle largely alone to protect their children from drug use, involvement in crime or gangs, prison, and debilitating injury and/or death. Amid these threats, and considering the lack of strong and trustworthy institutional or community support systems, violence may appear like the only possible intervention when they perceive their children are spiraling out of control. Here, being the only available way of solving a problem, physical aggression takes, again, the form of a repertoire of action.

GLIMMERS OF HOPE

A full account of the array of actions residents of Arquitecto Tucci undertake to cope with surrounding violence would not be complete if we fail to account for more collective, organized, and nonviolent efforts. The organization Mothers Against Paco is comprised of a small but active group of mothers whose sons and daughters are addicted to freebase cocaine. They have been active in the neighborhood since 2004 when, according to one of its founding members, Isabel, they began to "notice these kids, all dirty, without much clothing, walking like zombies." At the time, Isabel was the coordinator of a soup kitchen and was unfamiliar with the physical and psychological effects of paco, the drug to which many of these zombielike kids were addicted. Through engagement with basic research and meetings with authorities and physicians, Isabel and her neighbors, in a kind of grassroots collective action that resembled those organized around environmental pollutants, quickly became skilled at absorbing scientific knowledge (Brown 1991; Brown et al. 2000).

The violence triggered by drug dealing and consumption did not escape Isabel and her neighbors' notice, and the group soon began to organize protests against the presence of dealers in their neighborhoods. In an innovative move, the members of Mothers Against Paco began engaging in public shaming (locally known as *escraches*) of drug dealers by marching around dealers' houses, denouncing the deleterious effects of the product dealers were selling, and demanding court action. "At the beginning," Isabel remembers, "it was just three or four of us . . . but then, we grew . . . in the last *escrache*, we were more than one hundred . . . the judge took notice and issued a search warrant."

Peaceful collective action is also directed against the authorities, and, in particular, the police, who are seen as complicit with the violence that impacts the area. To conclude this chapter, let us describe one specific instance of such community action. On February 13, 2013, a group of two dozen residents of Arquitecto Tucci attended a meeting called by community organizers, activists from the Movimiento Evita (a faction of the governing Peronist Party), and by Mothers Against Paco. The meeting was called after the murder of sixty-three-year-old resident Luciano Tolaba. Tolaba resisted a robbery—believed to have been initiated by three young adults under the influence of drugs and/or alcohol—and was punched and stoned to death as a result.[5]

The explicit purpose of the meeting organized in the aftermath of Tolaba's death was to demand greater protection from the local police precinct. But the meeting also served as an arena for residents to vent their frustrations with police complicity with drug dealers and police inaction in the face of increasing violence in the neighborhood. What was said there (and screamed and chanted at the rally two days later) shows that overwhelming violence has the potential to unite residents as it becomes collectively defined as a contentious political issue. The following field note is representative of the sorts of conversations that took place at the community meeting and, later, at the rally:

February 16, 2013. Nerina, a grassroots activist, opens the meeting and attempts to summarize the impetus for the gathering: "There have been many deaths in the neighborhood recently, and the police are nowhere to be found . . . there are a lot of kids who are consuming paco, and lots of *transas* [drug dealers]." Isabel, the most outspoken leader of Mothers Against Paco, shares: "Things are quite messed up. I do not want more police, or *mano dura* . . . I want the police to do their job. We all know where the *transas* are . . . we have insecurity because the kids who are on drugs steal in order to buy." Alicia, another leader of Mothers Against Paco, begins to speak about police complicity with dealers: "They know where they are but they don't do anything." It is then the turn of Elisa, a fifty-year-old woman whose son has recently been murdered. In a low, trembling voice, she clearly elaborates the problem they are all facing: "My son was killed because of a fight between two groups that wanted to control the area. We all know who killed him, but the state prosecutor wants witnesses. And who is going to be a witness? The kids [who know] are afraid because they know that the cops are complicit with the dealers. Nobody wants to talk, nobody wants to report. Everybody knows who killed my son, but nobody talks."

For about an hour, those at the meeting shared stories about their concerns with sons or daughters who are addicted to paco, pills, and/or alcohol ("Many, many times, I gave him money so that he could buy drugs . . . because I don't want him to be around stealing. I never told him the money was for drugs, but I knew . . . I just don't want him to be killed trying to get money to buy"), and about police protection or complicity ("I asked one of the dealers if he wasn't afraid of the cops . . . and he looked at me and said that you just have to bribe them"). The phrase "liberated zone" (*zona liberada*) is repeatedly uttered, conveying both widespread knowledge about police complicity and also a generalized feeling of being "unprotected." As the meeting came to a close, attendees agreed on the main claim they would make in the rally that would proceed two days later: "We want the police and the courts to fulfill their role. No more liberated zones. Those who consume should not go to jail, dealers should be imprisoned." The flyers calling residents to the rally summarized their point of view: "Enough drugs and deaths in our community. No more liberated zones."

Friday, February 18. Approximately eighty residents march through the streets of Tucci carrying placards that read "No

FIGURE 28. Rally.

more liberated zones" and chant songs that claim "Justice for Tolaba." Residents gather peacefully in front of the local precinct demanding protection and police action against drug dealers. An eight-year-old carries a sign that, I believe, encapsulates the fear and impotence that overwhelms Tucci's residents: "I'm growing up in a neighborhood full of drugs and criminals. What do I do?" (figures 28 and 29).

Although not definite, part of the answer to the question posed by this eight-year-old is in the very process in which he is participating: an emergent social movement. True, it may seem contradictory to demand protection from a state that is widely perceived to be producing the violence that constitutes the residents' main grievance. But incongruities rarely stop collective action. Listening to mothers tell stories of their "search" for their "disappeared" children—children, they understand, they "lost" to paco—and witnessing how they are

FIGURE 29. "I am growing up in a neighborhood full of drugs and criminals. What do I do?"

organizing to make claims on the state in a context of widespread arbitrariness and fear, we couldn't help but think of other mothers in Argentina and elsewhere who, in the not too distant past, engaged in analogous actions (Bouvard 1994; Arditti 1999). We are not implying a similarity between the incipient Mothers Against Paco and what has arguably been the most powerful and effective social movement in recent Argentine history, the Mothers of the Plaza de Mayo (although the former is certainly inspired by the latter). What we do suggest is that one answer to "What do I do?" maybe (hopefully) lies in a successful model of organizing and claim making laid out by the human rights movement more than three decades ago.

TOWARD A POLITICAL SOCIOLOGY OF URBAN MARGINALITY

March 2011. Today I'm on door duty. I welcome students at the school gate. Briana, my student from last year, arrives at 12:40. We hug. I ask her how she is doing, as the last time we saw each other, she told me about Manuel, her brother who was killed on Christmas day. Briana is very small, and she talks in a very soft, sweet voice. "My father is not doing well. He is a mess; he saw everything. It all happened around 6:00 a.m. The bullet was not for Manuel, it was for Roque, a friend of my brother. Roque is tall, and my brother is like you . . . a dwarf! They were all fighting, they were drunk. Manuel was behind Roque, that's why the bullet went into his heart. It scratched Roque's shoulder. My mother is going to blow up a picture of Manuel and put it on his tomb." Briana leaves, and Jaira and Elisabeth say hi to me. They are in fourth grade. I ask them about their brother, who was shot a few days ago and is in intensive care at the local hospital. "He is a little bit better; he has a hole in his neck; the doctors did it [a tracheotomy]. They say he will be okay."

Excerpt from Fernanda's diary

Oftentimes during fieldwork, we had doubts about what our proper response would be (what were *we* to do?) to stories like this and to the many others presented in this book. Fernanda, for example, wrote in her diary: "I didn't search for these stories, but one day I began to listen to them all at once, inside the classroom. And it's been two years since I began to write them down, three academic cycles. And I still do not know what to tell my students when they describe the pain they feel when someone dies, or when another one ends up in the hospital, or when a close relative goes to jail." Listening to them attentively and with respect, faithfully recording what she heard, hugging them, and crying with them when they expressed their sorrow was the way in which Fernanda attempted to "answer them." Fernanda, an elementary schoolteacher, has an intuitive understanding of the fieldworker's primary commitment. As Scheper-Hughes writes, "Seeing, listening, touching, recording, can be, if done with care and sensitivity, acts of fraternity and sisterhood, acts of solidarity. Above all, they are the work of recognition. Not to look, not to touch, not to record, can be the hostile act, the act of indifference and of turning away" (1992:28). But we also slowly and jointly began to convince ourselves that another "answer" was the writing of this book, which, in its most basic sense, is a report on Tucci residents' daily predicaments, a public archive that stores their experiences of suffering and ethical coping.

As we made clear at the beginning of this book, we restricted our definition of violence to the actions that intentionally threaten to harm, intend to harm, or effectively harm other people. Our emphasis on physical harm does not ignore other very significant harmful effects that violence has. Take the case of rape, for example. As Jackman points out, the psychological and social injuries produced by a rape might be even more important than the physical damage: a rape is fundamentally an attack on sexual autonomy, which brings "in its trail personal humiliation, sense of violation, loss of control, anxiety, and frequently social shame" (2002:394). Nor does our focus on violent interpersonal interactions ignore the key relevance of the general social and political conditions under which the stories presented above unfold. The violence we examined is not the product of deviant individual behavior but of a larger context, one that scholars such as Paul Farmer and Philippe Bourgois would undoubtedly characterize as "structural violence."

In his celebrated theoretical treatise on violence, Randall Collins proposes bringing together different forms of interpersonal aggression under one theoretical roof in order to identify common situational and emotional dynamics. As he writes:

> If we zero in on the situation of interaction—the angry boyfriend with the crying baby, the armed robber squeezing the trigger on the holdup victim, the cop beating up the suspect—we can see patterns of confrontation, tension, and emotional flow which are at the heart of the situation where violence is carried out . . . [T]he situation of fear and tension gets resolved into a minority who ride the wave of fear, and a majority who are swept along by it. (2008:2, 57)

We are ambivalent about the virtue, the analytical payoff, of thinking along theoretically analogical lines about a pillow fight and a riot (to mention two phenomena touched upon by Collins, the former with which we are both familiar as parents and the latter with which one of us is familiar as a sociologist [Auyero 2007]). As students of both interpersonal and collective violence, we are also quite doubtful about the kind of bracketing of background conditions Collins proposes in order to construct a microsociological theory of violence. The "before people arrive in a situation of confrontation" is, we believe, crucial in shaping both the mechanics and the meanings of violence (see, for example, Contreras 2012). Conceptions of violence are contingent upon time and place, and the exercise of individual and collective violence sometimes expresses joint notions of pride, respect, and dignity (Schneider and Schneider 2003; Bourgois 1995; Armstrong 1998; Blok 2001; Kakar 1996). Agnosticism and doubts aside, we want to emphasize once more that as valuable as a general theory of violence could be for other purposes, we did not immerse in the particular social universe of Arquitecto Tucci in order to emerge with a set of more or less generalizable or more or less robust theoretical connections between different forms of violence. The moment we intuited that the domestic fight could be related to the dispute between the dealer and consumer, or that the attempted rape could be connected to the attack on a neighbor's house, we began—both obsessively and systematically—to trace the concrete, empirical links between them. The question we sought to answer through our empirical material was a fairly straightforward one: How and why are the different and seemingly unrelated types of violence that overwhelm poor people's daily lives associated in real time and space? Our empirical question was, as we stated in the introduction, guided by a set of theoretical concerns about the actual operation of what other scholars call the "continuum of violence," and about the need to move beyond the rigid boundaries between different kinds of violence. Consequently, our main question had, right from the beginning, large potential analytical implications: if we were right about the concatenated character of interpersonal harm, then current ways of approaching interpersonal violence might need to be modified.

Many social scientists have speculated, and occasionally empirically examined, relationships between systems of oppression, injustice, and interpersonal violence. With a more expansive definition of violence than the one adopted here, scholars such as Moser and McIlwaine (2004) have noted the connections between social, economic, and political violence, and Scheper-Hughes and Bourgois (2003) have inspected the links between structural, symbolic, everyday, and intimate forms of violence. Our effort, inspired by the call to unearth hidden relationships, but dictated by an empirically based intuition, took a different track: first, we restricted our definition of violence to intentional perpetration of interpersonal harm and second, we explored the lateral connections between diverse forms of violence without considering some as more meaningful or relevant than others (Hume 2009).

During the course of our fieldwork, we often thought that violence was akin to an oil spill. A human-produced form of pollution, the release of crude oil into the environment can come from many sources (a tanker, a drilling rig, an offshore platform), and although it can be controlled by different methods, it can also have quick, devastating effects on the environment and on living beings. It is not hard to see why, when collecting and analyzing our data, the image of an oil spill constantly appeared in our minds. Originating in diverse interactions, violence seemed to be seeping through the social fabric, touching the lives of many, including those not directly involved in it.[1] Although evocative of the rugged character that everyday life has in the neighborhood, we chose the less ambiguous notion of concatenation to highlight the very concrete linkages between one form of violence and another.

It is impossible for us to say "how much" of the violence in the neighborhood takes the concatenated form that the material presented above well illustrates—we simply do not know how many of the street fights, the sexual attacks inside and outside homes, the domestic disputes, or the murders are part of a longer sequence of events. What we do know is that a thorough account of violence at the urban margins cannot focus exclusively on discrete episodes (be they murders, street fights, sexual attacks, etc.). The main finding of this book—and the chief invitation to other researchers and scholars interested in the subject—is that diverse forms of violence not only accumulate in poor neighborhoods but also concatenate. If we are to avoid distorting—and somewhat disfiguring—the actual dynamics of interpersonal violence at the urban margins, we not only need to pay attention to the piling up of diverse forms of intentional physical harm but also to the ways in which they relate to one another in the lives of the most dispossessed.

Two of our main sources of theoretical inspiration for this analysis have been Norbert Elias and Charles Tilly. In the view of Elias's *The Civilizing Process*, there is a strong link between long-term structural development in society and long-term changes in people's social relations and social character (what he calls their "social habitus"). In the view of Tilly's *The Contentious French*, in turn, there is a deep connection between large-scale processes, such as state making and repertoires of collective action. Throughout the pages of this book, we have attempted an analogous analytic effort: to simultaneously examine diachrony and synchrony by focusing on forms of violence (concatenation) and its trans*form*ation (depacification). One of the key dimensions in Elias's civilizing, pacifying process is the "lengthening of chains of social action and interdependence" (1994: 448) among individuals and groups, which yields greater predictability in social life. The violent concatenations described in this book, and "the perpetual proximity of danger" (ibid. 449) they entail, produce the opposite effect. Despite people's best-intended efforts at "making toast," social life becomes more unpredictable and insecure. We are thus able to see the theoretical links between depacification and concatenated violence and the way in which they unfold on Tucci's rough ground.

It is not hard to imagine the medium- and long-term consequences of growing up and living in a hostile place like Arquitecto Tucci. Plenty of research has shown that chronic exposure to violence not only affects physical health and safety but also psychological functioning, emotional well-being, academic achievement, moral development, and a whole array of social relations (Schwab-Stone et al. 1995; Margolin and Gordis 2000; Guerra, Huesman, and Spindler 2003; Brennan, Molnar, and Earls 2007; Farrell et al. 2007; McCart et al. 2007; Walton, Harris, and Davidson 2009). Exposure to violence (homicide, in particular) also affects children's behavior and cognitive performance in more immediate ways (Sharkey 2010; Sharkey et al. 2012). Furthermore, from studies in psychology, we know that histories of violent victimization or previous aggression are the best predictors of domestic violence: children who have witnessed violent interactions between parents have a higher risk of being involved in violent interactions within the household, either as victims or as perpetrators. In order to understand the intergenerational transmission of violence, scholars typically resort to explanations that revolve around "social learning." Children exposed to physical aggression among caretakers might come to believe that violence is an accepted and/or effective way to deal with conflict and might thus be inclined to use violence (Ehrensaft et al. 2003; Fosco et al. 2007; Voisin et al. 2011; DeBoard-Lucas and Grych 2011). Or, as Jennifer Friday puts it, "Children who observe violence at home may learn that violence is a way of communicating and a way of dealing with life's everyday issues—a way of relating to others" (1995:403).

Either as a mechanism to confront stressful situations or as a method to attempt to solve problems (or both), violence is learned, either directly or indirectly. Although our analytical attention has focused on the factors that produce and reproduce this chronic and overwhelming violence, and on the uses and concatenated forms of interpersonal aggression in the here and now, this scholarship forces us to think about the long-term effects of this violence. Perhaps here it might be useful to recall Pierre Bourdieu when, in his masterful *Pascalian Meditations*, he asserts that we are disposed because we are exposed. The following paragraph seems to have been written with highly violent sociosymbolic universes such as Tucci in mind:

> It is because the body is (to unequal degrees) exposed and endangered in the world, faced with the risk of emotion, lesion, suffering, sometimes death, and therefore obliged to take the world seriously (and nothing is more serious than emotion, which touches the depths of our organic being) that it is able to acquire dispositions that are themselves an openness to the world, that is, to the very structures of the social world of which they are incorporated form. (2000:141)

What kind of schemes of action, perception, and evaluation, we should then ask, are being forged while being routinely exposed to this harsh environment? What type of habitus emerges out of constantly living in harm's way? The daily knowledge that allows marginalized residents to navigate a threatening social world in a more or less competent fashion is "an incarnate, sensuous, situated 'knowing-how-to' that operates beneath the controls of discursive awareness and propositional reasoning" (Wacquant 2005:466). Although we touched upon this theme with the notion of repertoire, we believe that we only began to scratch the surface of a much deeper issue. As with all social agents, those dwelling at the urban margins are embodied and emplaced actors, and their social life "rests on a bedrock of visceral know-how, or prediscursive knowledges and skills that are both acquired and deployed in practical entailment" (Wacquant 2005:467) with that particular dangerous spatial universe. We thus not only need to understand and explain how people use, think, and talk about violence but also how they *embody* and *sense* it. Loïc Wacquant's carnal ethnography (2005; see also Desmond 2010) and Katherine Geurts's anthropology of the senses (2003) provide useful theoretical and methodological tools for such a scholarly endeavor.

It is now time to step back from the ethnographic details (or the dots, in the pointillistic analogy we referred to at the beginning of this book) and examine the (bigger) empirical and analytical picture. Regarding the first, what explains violence at the urban margins? Regarding the second, what can the analysis presented here contribute toward a political sociology of urban marginality?

As in many other urban areas in Latin America, the violence dissected here has a lot to do with high levels of social inequality feeding truly unequal life chances. The coexistence of extreme marginality and fabulous wealth that now characterizes countries like Argentina (Svampa 2001; Pirez 2001) is also at the root of the increase in violence, and so are the "fragile legitimacy of the state monopoly of violence . . . widespread deficits in the rule of law, and . . . extensive corruption among the police" (Imbusch, Misse, and Carrión 2011). But factors more specific to Buenos Aires, and to Arquitecto Tucci, also help us to understand and explain the depacification of relegated territories in urban Argentina and the specific forms and meanings violence takes there. Prominent among them are the expansion of the illicit drug trade, particularly its location in poor urban zones, and the informalization of the economy. As illicit drug trade increased, so did the systemic violence that is inherent in this type of illegal market. As the economy progressively informalized, violence also became a major regulatory mechanism of social relations. La Salada, the specific spatial configuration that the informalization of the economy takes in Arquitecto Tucci, adds a special element ("seasoning," in the police chief's apt wording) to the violence in the area. As violent specialists monopolized the exercise of violence (and charged taxes in exchange for protection), the market eventually became pacified, but violence was "exported"—in the form of opportunistic crime—to the immediate adjacencies of *la feria*. Many of the violent episodes described above can be traced back to "drugs" and "La Salada." Others, such as the many instances of physical disputes between residents (some of them resulting in serious bodily harm) over the geographic limits of their properties, can be traced back to the informalization of poor people's access to land illustrated in the rapid proliferation of squatter settlements (Cravino et al. 2008).

But once we expand the scope of our analysis and focus on the concatenations of violence (concatenations that include dyadic retaliations but do not conclude in them), the span of our explanation and understanding should also be enlarged. To make better sense of concatenated violence (and the individual and collective actions it generates), we also need to pay attention to state actions and inactions, such as police arbitrariness and brutality, police participation in diverse forms of criminality (such as the drug trade), and the almost total (and patriarchal) institutional disregard for—and occasional complicity with—domestic and sexual violence. Virulent policing alongside the routine incarceration of poor youth, together with police involvement in various illegal activities (car theft and drug trafficking, for example) prove that the state is not exterior to this maelstrom of violence. The insecurity of precarious populations is in fact aggravated, not attenuated, by the intervention of purported "law enforcement" offices.[2]

Economic *and* political forces are thus at the root of the whirlpool of violence that wreaks havoc in Tucci's daily life. To point accusing fingers exclusively at economic "neoliberalism"—and the attendant rise of inequality, unemployment, and massive degradation in poor people's lives—would be a huge and misleading simplification. Similarly, to solely blame state actors' participation in crime for the explosion of interpersonal violence would leave out the operation of forces such as the neo-liberal informalization of the economy. State actors, we should also note, do not only produce violence through their illicit participation in crime but the state's failure to act, its selective outright neglect, is also a key factor. In fact, many times during the course of our fieldwork, and also during the analysis of the hundreds of pages of field notes and interviews, we asked ourselves: What would have happened if a trusted state official (a police officer, a school counselor, a social worker) had intervened somewhere along the violent sequence of events? And the speculative answer was always the same: the increasing violence of the interactions would have de-escalated. That this seldom happened helps us to better understand the persistence of violence in this particular territory.

Seen from urban margins, the state is sometimes complicit with crime (making deals with dealers, liberating zones for delinquency, recruiting youngsters for criminal activity, etc.). Other times it is the agent who carries out the harassment, punishment, or execution (as when it intimidates poor youngsters, incarcerates them, or kills and/or injures them as in the case of "trigger-happy" cops). Other times it is the state that looks the other way ("averts its gaze," as Scheper-Hughes [1992] would put it) and neglects or abandons them (as when it fails to aid youngsters and adults who were recently released from prison, lacks well-funded and staffed rehab centers for drug addicts, etc.).[3]

Factors external to the space of the neighborhood help to explain the violence within it. But we would be deaf and blind to our evidence if we denied residents' key participation in the perpetuation of interpersonal physical harm. After all, most perpetrators of violence do not come from outside Tucci but live inside the neighborhood. Here, the notion of repertoire helps us to make sense of how, for many in Tucci, violence is a routine way of addressing pressing daily problems. This repertoire, it should be emphasized, is not endogenously generated, but it has been forged in the entanglement between this relegated area and the above-mentioned outside factors. Forces external to the neighborhood, together with a repertoire that is sustained and reproduced by Tucci residents, help to explain the perpetuation of interpersonal physical harm in daily interactions.

We do not want to leave the reader with the impression that Arquitecto Tucci encapsulates the recent history of Argentina. Tucci is not the country's current predicament writ small. No place can accomplish that. What our analysis of daily violence in one specific social universe reveals, however, is both a series of the uses and forms that violence takes and the economic and political forces at their root. In addition, our analysis presents, implicitly by way of empirical demonstration rather than in the explicit form of an analytic blueprint, one more step toward the kind of political sociology of urban marginality that one of us has been attempting to construct for two decades (Auyero 2000, 2007, 2012). At a very basic level, this political sociology proposes that when studying popular politics (clientelism, insurgency, violent collective action, or poor people's waiting, to name the aspects that one of us has been paying most of his attention to), we need to engage in a double, objective and subjective, reading because sociopolitical phenomena live double lives: for patronage, in the distribution of resources and votes, and in the experiences of clients, brokers, and patrons; for protest, in public performances, opportunities, and networks, and in the perspectives of participants in collective actions; for waiting, in the measurable time poor folks are forced to endure in line to receive benefits from the state; and in the way in which they make sense of this waiting. And the same goes for violence at the urban margins. We cannot stop at murder rates or body counts. We need to dissect the forms violence takes and the meanings violence has for both victims and perpetrators.

Urban sociology in the United States has demonstrated how public policies can accelerate or deter a neighborhood's downward spiral (Massey and Denton 1993; Venkatesh 2000; Logan 2003; Sampson 2012; Sharkey 2013), and many works have dissected the specific effects that the presence or absence of public services and state programs can make in the life (and death) of the urban poor (Adams 2013; Klinenberg 2008; Wacquant 2007). Spurred by the contemporary gargantuan expansion of the prison system and the concentration of this massive growth among specific racial and ethnic groups in urban areas, recent scholarship has also begun to pay sustained and systematic attention to the ways in which the unprecedented level of mass incarceration is also affecting everyday life in poor communities (Goffman 2009; Comfort 2008; Rios 2010) and the children of incarcerated parents in particular (Murray et al. 2009).[4] This strand of urban research clearly shows that the concentration of crime in a neighborhood, the decrepit character of its housing, residents' exposure to environmental hazards and their attendant poor health, are all outcomes of decisions made outside the neighborhood—they are the product of government action and inaction. In other words, the more or less marginalized character of a neighborhood is far from a "natural" phenomena but the consequence of a deeply political process. Given how central state power is in the misfortunes experienced by marginalized places and peoples such as Arquitecto Tucci (Logan and Molotch 1987; Sharkey 2013), public policy (or its absence in the form of neglect) should be a key subject in the political sociology of urban marginality.

Examining the causes of persistent African American poverty in the United States, sociologist Patrick Sharkey states that "[a]ny approach to addressing the problems arising in neighborhoods of concentrated poverty must begin with the recognition that the social problems that characterize poor, segregated urban neighborhoods have not arisen because of any character deficiencies of low-income African Americans or other ethnic minorities. The problems have emerged due to a combination of economic and political disinvestment in urban neighborhoods, along with social policies that served to exacerbate the challenges of economic dislocation faced by poor communities" (2013:573). Sharkey identifies four elements at the root of durable inequality in urban neighborhoods in the United States: "1) the failure to complete the progression toward full civil rights; 2) the implementation of a diverse set of policies, informal strategies, and institutional mechanisms used to maintain racial inequality in urban areas; 3) the restructuring of urban labor markets; and 4) the destructive response to economic dislocation in America's cities" (ibid. 973). His analysis is useful because it points to conjoining economic and political forces in the production and reproduction of urban marginality and persistent inequality. As we saw in chapter 1, in the absence of well-funded, comprehensive, sustained urban policy (other than tenure regulation and a few infrastructural projects in parts of the neighborhood, not much has been done in the area), the overall fate of the urban poor in Tucci (and in many other low-income neighborhoods) has been mainly driven by economic transformations. Deindustrialization deprived the neighborhood of a stable economic base, and then, in the early 1990s, the mainstay of economic subsistence in the neighborhood began to be provided by the highly exploitative, unregulated, informal market of La Salada.

Formal policy decisions do have an impact in the lives of the dispossessed—in Tucci and elsewhere. But two and a half years of fieldwork—and, in the case of one of us, two decades of studying poor people's lives—have taught us to take these with a healthy degree of skepticism. Of course, the ongoing Supreme Court mandated cleanup of the highly contaminated Riachuelo River is important for those living adjacent to it (Auyero 2012), but so is the fact that a lot of the highly toxic debris extracted in the process ends up leveling the ground of the new squatter settlement (because, as we learned, truck drivers—probably with the complicity of the company in charge of transporting the sludge and of municipal officials—agree, for pay, to dump their content closer to the river instead of taking it to a treatment plant). Of course, the free provision of laptops to schoolchildren, which the federal government put into place, is important, but so is the fact that the school does not have a single wireless router to connect them (a fact that we learned when the school principal asked us, and we agreed, to purchase a few). Of course, the opening of a new health center is important, but so is the fact that many times we had to go to the emergency room with one of the schoolchildren, basic supplies (for stitching up an open wound on a ten-year-old boy's head, for example) were missing.

Neighborhoods of relegation across Latin America are not only affected by formal state initiatives (infrastructural projects, housing policies, welfare programs, etc.) but also by the operation of informal institutions, and prominent among them is clientelism. Politicians' and state officials' personalized distribution of goods and services in search of votes and/or participants for a political machine is, seen from the bottom up, one of the few available ways in which the poor relationally solve their daily survival problems (Auyero 2000). Although a veritable cottage industry on the topic (with a curious epicenter in Argentina and Peronism in particular) has emerged during the last decade (Calvo y Murillo 2004; Stokes 2005; Weitz-Shapiro 2006; Giraudy 2007; Szwarcberg 2010), much more still needs to be scrutinized concerning the emergence, strengthening, and legitimation of this way of doing politics and this way of solving pressing problems among the poor. The operation of clientelism—and of other informal institutions (Helmke and Levitsky 2004)—should also be a chapter in the political sociology of urban marginality.

Describing the cycle of mobilization that swept through Rio de Janeiro's favelas between the late 1970s and mid-1980s, historian Bryan McCann writes that "favela activists led a movement to bridge the long-standing divide between favelas and the formal city in Rio de Janeiro. They challenged the practices that had long consigned favela residents to difficult lives—insecurity of land tenure, limited access to formal employment and public education, and the expectation of routine harassment by the forces of law and order—demanding equal rights to the city" (2014:15). This statement highlights another phenomena that, central to any political analysis of urban marginality, has remained largely absent in many studies of poor neighborhoods in urban scholarship in the United States (see Pellow [2002] for an exception) but, in contrast, has been a quite prominent feature in urban studies in the global south: popular protest and neighborhood activism, or "insurgent citizenship" in anthropologist James Holston's phrase (Holston 2008; McCann 2014). From the "quiet encroachment of the ordinary" examined by Asef Bayat (1997) to the open, more or less transgressive forms of collective action (Castells 1984; Lazar 2008), popular mobilization figures conspicuously in almost every historical and ethnographic account of poor Latin American neighborhoods because it has been a crucial phenomenon in triggering, conditioning, and/or limiting state actions, and thus in shaping poor people's living conditions.

The analysis presented above also tells us that a political sociology of urban marginality should be attuned to the variety of forms that policing takes in the space where the dispossessed and vulnerable populations dwell: a militarized and incarcerating iron fist in poor areas of Mexico (Müller 2012); a terrorizing raid, as in the barrios of Managua (Rodgers 2006:325); a police-criminal "collusion" of the kind described by Arias (2006) in Rio de Janeiro's favelas; or, as the contemporary Conurbano Bonaerense shows, a sometimes maddening coexistence and overlapping of fists, raids, and collusion.

The kind of political sociology of urban marginality we advocate should take into account the less official and less public state actions—and the interactions that ensue. These should also be the foci of empirical attention, because they are crucial explanatory dimensions of what goes on at the urban margins. To give two contemporary examples: Wouldn't it be unreasonable to try to understand and explain daily life in Soacha, a *comuna* on the outskirts of Bogotá, without factoring in the existence of former and current paramilitary forces and their "social cleansing" campaigns targeting poor youths, their obscure links with established political actors, and the presence of drug traffickers? Would it be realistic to approach everyday life in Tubarão or Vigário Geral, two favelas in Rio de Janeiro, without simultaneously taking into consideration the illicit relationships between drug traffickers, politicians, and police forces? The examples could multiply (see Dewey 2012; McCann 2014). Clandestine connections between established political actors and more or less organized perpetrators of violence count in the everyday production of urban marginality in Latin America and should be part of any understanding of existing political dynamics. The obvious fact that these are less easily codable—and the outcome of a research based on them, less susceptible to being formalized—should not dictate the epistemic preference for less "messy" data.[5]

The condition of contemporary marginalized territories and populations is the product of not always visible, not always measurable, and not always licit relations. Part of our analysis has centered on the ones established between police forces and some individuals and groups engaged in crime—but what, in another work, one of us calls "the gray zone of state power" (Auyero 2007) comprises other kinds of illicit relationships.

Decades of urban research in Latin America tell us that a political sociology of urban marginality would not be possible without a serious consideration of informal institutions. The same goes, we believe, for clandestine connections between established political actors, the forces of law and order, and perpetrators of violence.

The fate of marginalized spaces should thus be examined as the product of a particular, historically contingent interaction between macrostructural economic forces, state policies, and the active engagement of marginalized populations—as individuals and sometimes through collective organizations—with those external pressures. Rather than concentrating on the properties of the populations trapped in relegated neighborhoods, a relational perspective on the production of urban marginality needs to have, as its primary empirical foci, policies *and* discourses, structures *and* experiences, forms *and* connections, the economy *and* the state. The pernicious forms of "willful" governmentality parents engage in as they involve corrupt police officials in the disciplining of their children demonstrate the state's deep implication both "in the minute texture of [poor people's] everyday life" (Gupta 1995:375) and in the subjectivities of the dispossessed. Attention to the daily manufacturing of political authority and of political subjectivities, through the systematic scrutiny of *state practices* (actual encounters between state and citizens), is also a necessary component of the political sociology of the urban margins. Focusing on state practices complicates arguments about the presence or absence of the state and directs our attention to instances of state-citizen interactions that link the daily state operation (formal and informal, legal and illegal) with the lives of the subordinated. Being central to the routine construction of the state and to the shared understandings of what the state does and is, these everyday encounters give "concrete shape and form to what would otherwise be an abstraction ('the state')" (Gupta 1995:378).

If our analysis is correct, that is, if different forms of violence are much more entangled than the dyadic retaliation approach would allow us to see, then any public policy that seeks to address widespread interpersonal violence in the area should, if it is to be successful, be integrative. In other words, if much of the violence comes in a concatenated form, so should responses to it. Angélica should not have to travel an hour and a half outside the neighborhood to seek treatment for her addicted son and then spend another hour in a different direction to seek protection from domestic violence; nor should she wait endlessly for a counselor to guide her in shielding her younger children from the violence that surrounds them. In the face of interrelated violences, drug therapy, treatment, mediation, conciliation, and law enforcement should come together, at the same time, in the same space. The seemingly intractable persistence of interpersonal violence in Buenos Aires might find the beginnings of a solution (or, at least, a model to emulate) in an unlikely place: Colombia's Casas de Justicia (Houses of Justice). Located in poor communities, the Casas de Justicia gather various welfare, legal, and social institutions (from legal advisors and police to family services and specialists on drug addiction) under one roof, thus facilitating access to justice, mediation, and treatment for the poor.[6] The Casas de Justicia are neither the only integrative approach to community violence (for organizations, see Bloom's "sanctuary model" [1997, 2003]) nor a cure-all solution (and some may find them, in fact, functional to the neoliberal vision of justice administration; see, for example, Rodríguez and Uprimny 2014). But they might provide a blueprint for those seeking to lessen the violence that currently overwhelms the lives of those at the bottom of the sociosymbolic order. But this quite modest "policy recommendation" remains vacuous if the larger issue—that of the state's clandestine participation in the production of violence—remains unaddressed.

For the past decade, many Latin American governments have experienced a "post-neoliberal left turn," placing the reduction of inequality and the alleviation of poverty at the center of public discourse and, to a lesser extent, policy making (Lavinas 2013). The novel progressive consensus suggests that citizenship (and democracy) cannot survive without the "social inclusion" of the masses of marginalized individuals that, according to the now dominant diagnosis, were cast aside by decades of neoliberal economic policies. Addressing what both moderate and radical governments in the subcontinent call the "drama of social exclusion" requires the intense action of the welfare arm of the state, not only the (more or less clientelist, more or less empowering, more or less effective) cash transfer programs now in vogue but also the expansion of the provision of decommodified services such as education, sanitation, housing, and public health.[7]

Consistent with trends identified by other scholars in many countries in the subregion, the analysis presented above should make clear that without the pacification of everyday life in marginalized communities, even the meager "social inclusion" purportedly enacted by social assistance programs is at risk of becoming an empty panacea. In other words, at a time when official discourse, both in Argentina and in other "pink tide" countries in Latin America, calls for more state intervention—counteracting decades of neoliberal state retrenchment—the rollout of the welfare state should be accompanied with the reining in of the illicit and belligerent arm that by now constitutes a main source of dislocation in poor people's lives.

ACKNOWLEDGMENTS

We are truly grateful to Fernanda's students and to the staff at the schools where she worked for allowing us to conduct our research, in particular to the principal, vice principal, and the coordinator of the *gabinete social*.

Fernanda wishes to thank her friends, Paula Weintraub and Laura Pagés. They were there to listen to her while this book was in the making, and they supported her in the effort to "document suffering." Thanks also to Sandra de Alva and to her fellow teachers and the school personnel.

Vany Collins first alerted us to the existence of basic data on interpersonal violence. Thanks to Majo Ripa for leading us to Vany, and to Vany for starting our adventure through the local hospitals. Fernando Navarro put us in touch with the directors and doctors of the main local hospital. They devoted time to us, which they usually lack, to talk about a mutual concern. Special thanks to Juan Ignacio for sharing his detailed study of trauma and surgery. Thanks to Leyla Mesyngier who helped us during the first interviews at local hospitals and to Marcelo Sain who provided us with criminal data. Ariel Dulitzky, University of Texas (UT) law professor at UT-Austin, put us in touch with Germán Bauche, who provided us with crucial data on homicides in Arquitecto Tucci. Ariel Budnik and Daniel Fridman (Javier's colleague at UT) helped us to figure out basic demographic data (we wish we could thank the

INDEC, the national institute of statistics, but they couldn't—or didn't want to—help us). Orla O'Sullivan-Roche, undergraduate student at UT, collaborated in the collection of secondary sources about crime and violence in Tucci. Thanks y'all. Young, energetic, and formidable "cronista," María Florencia Alcaraz, did a lot of the legwork for the section on the police in Tucci. Together with Javier, she wrote a piece, published in the online magazine *Anfibia*, that served as the basis for our analysis of the state (mis)interventions in the area. Gracias, Florencia! And thanks to Cristian Alarcón for putting us in touch and for unknowingly planting the seed of "a different way of writing" in us. Agustín Burbano de Lara deserves special thanks for his indefatigable fieldwork.

Colleagues at the Population Research Center at UT, particularly Kelly Ralley (who made us aware of critical distinctions within the literature on forms of violence against women) and Mark Warr (who pointed to relevant literature on effects of early exposure to violence), also deserve to be thanked. Daniel Brinks, in the UT Government Department, read a much shorter Spanish version of this text and criticized its "pointillistic" lack of general argument. We hope this version addresses his well-intended critique. We also owe special thanks to three of Javier's graduate students: Kristine Kilanski, Katherine Jensen, and Jacinto Cuvi. It was in dialogue with them that the arguments of chapters 2 and 4 were developed and sharpened.

As this book was taking shape, so was the Urban Ethnography Lab in the Sociology Department at UT. Kristine, Katie, and Jacinto are among the students who are making UT Sociology (and the Ethnography Lab in particular) an exciting, stimulating, and fun place to work. Thanks, then, to Katherine Sobering, Emily Spangenberg, Caitlyn Collins, Pamela Neumann, Jorge Derpic, Jessica Dunning-Lozano, Marcos Perez, and Esther Sullivan for comments, encouragement, and simply for being there, day in and day out, making intellectual work a truly collective enterprise. And, Christine Williams, former chair of the Sociology Department, Javier cannot thank you enough—not just for conceiving the lab and for the leave you granted to write this book but also, most important, for your endless intellectual support.

Katie Jensen (again), editor extraordinaire, *un millón de gracias* for working so hard and so diligently on our "rough ground" English. Javier Auyero presented parts of this book at the universities of British Columbia, Victoria, Rutgers, New York, Princeton, UC-Berkeley, North Carolina-Chapel Hill, Illinois-Chicago, South Florida, the London School of Economics, the Center for Latin American Studies at Cambridge University, the Instituto de Iberoamérica at the Universidad de Salamanca, and the New School for Social Research. He also presented preliminary versions at the Universidad de La Plata, the Universidad Nacional de San Martín (UNSAM), and the Collège de France. Immense thanks to participants for their comments and suggestions. A preliminary version of chapter 4 was presented at the Wenner-Gren Symposium "The Politics of the Urban Poor"; thanks to Veena Das and Shalini Randeria for organizing such a lively event—and the participants for their stimulating comments.

Matthew Desmond, Alice Goffman, Megan Comfort, Loïc Wacquant, Matthew Dewey, Margarethe Kusenbach, Nancy Scheper-Hughes, Carlos Forment, and Cristian Alarcón: we are extremely grateful for your criticism of and comments on drafts of different chapters. Philippe Bourgois, Randol Contreras, Andrew Deener, and David Smilde read the entire manuscript and provided enormously insightful and helpful criticism. *Gracias a los cuatro.* Dennis Rodgers read more versions of a few of the central chapters than many, and provided detailed and insightful suggestions. Thank you, Dennis!

Students in the graduate seminar "Poverty and Marginality in the Americas" first heard about the project and discussed a draft of one of the chapters. Thanks to Emily Spangenberg, Jennifer Scott, Natalie Richardson, Jorge Derpic, Jacinto Cuvi, Yu Chen, Ori Swed, Marcos Perez, Pamela Neumann, Kristine Kilanski, Caitlyn Collins, Katie Sobering, Michelle Mott, Elizabeth Velasquez, Erika Grajeda, and Daniel Jaster. Maybe you didn't notice it, but our conversations and debates were crucial contributions to this book. When we thought the book was done, Javier presented parts of it at a seminar at the Universidad de Rosario in Bogotá, Colombia. Thanks to participants and, in particular, to Thomas Ordóñez, Bastien Bosa, and Majo Álvarez Rivadulla for the unforgettable conversations and insightful suggestions, and, again, to Javier's *compañera de viaje*, anthropologist Nancy Scheper-Hughes, for her inestimable help to our way of thinking (and writing) about violence.

Eric Schwartz, Ryan Mulligan, and Cathy Slovensky at Princeton University Press—it's hard to think of a better editorial team. It's been a real pleasure working with you all. Part of this research was funded by the National Science Foundation (NSF Award SES-1153230), the Harry Frank Guggenheim Foundation, and by a grant from the Office of the Vice President for Research at the University of Texas at Austin. Funds were also provided by the Joe R. and Teresa Lozano Long Professorship and the Andrew W. Mellon Foundation Faculty Travel Grant given by the Teresa Lozano Long Institute of Latin American Studies (LLILAS). We cannot thank these funding agencies enough.

Earlier and shorter drafts of chapters 2 and 3 were published in the *Journal of Latin American Studies* and the *Journal of Contemporary Ethnography*. Thanks to the editors and reviewers for their helpful feedback and for permission to reproduce parts of them here.

METHODOLOGICAL APPENDIX

This book is based on an array of data production techniques: Fernanda's field diary, numerous and recurring ethnographic interviews conducted by Agustín Burbano de Lara (at the time of the fieldwork, a senior in the Sociology Department at the University of Buenos Aires), in-depth interviews with hospital and school staff conducted by the authors, in-depth interviews with police personnel conducted by professional journalist María Florencia Alcaraz, and one hundred short interviews with Tucci's residents conducted by Agustín and the authors. We also organized two photography workshops with elementary schoolchildren where they talked about what they liked and disliked about their neighborhood. Toward the end, Fernanda organized two focus groups with high school students (interview and focus group guides at the end of this appendix). We also analyzed available vital and criminal statistics and created a data set of homicides based on local newspaper reports.

Between April 2009 and August 2012—with the interruptions imposed by the winter and summer recesses—Fernanda registered in her field diary her activities as a teacher, the stories that her students brought to her, stories told by other teachers and school personnel, and stories told by students' parents. She always used pseudonyms to identify the main characters. At the beginning, we were interested in replicating the study of environmental suffering that one of us, together with anthropologist

Debora Swistun, carried out in the shantytown of Flammable (Auyero and Swistun 2009). Fernanda's students avidly talked about environmental risk, but most of their stories were about different types of violence. The hyperpresence of physical aggression in their stories made us reorient our study and refocus our attention on other sources of harm. At the beginning, violent episodes appeared to be isolated from one another. As we described earlier, a case of collective violence in response to a rape attempt alerted us to the possible connections between different forms of violence. From then on, we began to scrutinize possible linkages and complemented field notes with in-depth interviews. Agustín joined us as a research assistant during 2010 and 2011. He visited the neighborhood two or three times a week during six months and established a trusting relationship with the coordinators of one of the local soup kitchens. Through them, he got to know many other residents, first those attending the soup kitchen, then others through those residents. The interviews he conducted had a more informal character than the unidirectional exchange typical of research protocols and were conducted after weeks, and sometimes months, of mutual acquaintanceship. Agustín carried out what by now is understood as classic ethnographic work, that type of "social research based on the close-up, on-the-ground observation of people and institutions in real time and space, in which the investigator embeds herself near (or within) the phenomenon so as to detect how and why agents on the scene act, think and feel the way they do" (Wacquant 2003:5). Throughout the research, both in Fernanda's and Agustín's field notes and in the interviews, we applied the evidentiary criteria normally used for ethnographic research (Becker 1958, 1970; Katz 2001, 2002); higher evidentiary value was assigned to individual acts or patterns of conduct recounted by many observers than to those recounted by only one observer. Although particular in their details, the testimonies, field notes, and vignettes selected above represent behavior observed or heard about with consistent regularity during the course of our fieldwork.

In both the long and short interviews, we were interested in the same themes. Together with basic demographic data, we inquired about job history, participation in welfare programs, time of residence in the neighborhood, brief history of migration, comparison between past and present living conditions, and so on (see interview guides below). We paid particular attention to the way in which residents understood the main problems in the neighborhood, their sources, and possible solutions. When the issue of interpersonal violence emerged among adults with children, we asked them about their care practices, police presence in the area, and the role played by other neighborhood institutions (school, church, etc.). We also inquired about recreational spaces and participation in neighborhood associations.

Replicating a methodological strategy deployed in previous work (Auyero and Swistun 2009), we organized two photography workshops with sixth grade students at the local school. Agustín Burbano de Lara taught basic notions of photography, and as part of their final assignment, Fernanda asked them to take pictures of the neighborhood. They divided themselves into groups, and we gave them disposable cameras containing twenty-seven exposures each. They were told to take half of the pictures on things they liked about the neighborhood and half on things they did not like. We gave them no further instructions. They all returned the cameras, providing more than three hundred pictures. We talked with them about the things they intended to portray and the reasons why they liked or disliked a particular picture. When the time came to write this book, we selected the pictures that best represented the themes that were recurrent in both groups.

Toward the end of our fieldwork, we conducted in-depth interviews with local doctors and with personnel of the local police department; needless to say, the latter were not very insightful about actual (i.e., clandestine) police practices but did give us a good sense of the way in which police agents think about the local population. The interviews with doctors, on the other hand, were very helpful in identifying patterns of interpersonal violence (when violent episodes occur, changes over the last decade, etc.). The basic demographic data (household composition, employment, income, etc.) available at the municipal level is severely lacking and very poor—and quite worrisome. Our experiences varied greatly from US researchers who, with a few clicks of a mouse, can access data that it took us many months and many personal connections to get our hands on, such as basic data on homicides in the area. One ethnographic moment illustrates this point. After meeting a prominent local politician who, we were told, would facilitate access to data presumably available at the main local hospital, he put us in touch with the hospital director, who in turn recommended we talk with one of the ER chief surgeons. In the midst of his hectic days, this young doctor expressed his preoccupation with the complete absence of a reliable data set on emergency surgeries. He then told us that he was keeping his own record of surgeries performed at the emergency room (open and closed chest, due to car accidents, gunshots, etc.) and allowed us to photograph his notes (figure 30).

This doctor's sincere care and deep commitment notwithstanding, the precarious character of these essential statistics shows, in quite crystal clear form, utter state neglect. With the help of many doctors and with personnel at the local ombudsman office, we were able to reconstruct as best we could the objective profile of violence in the area. Limitations notwithstanding, we are as confident as we could be with the quality of our data. Given how many of the violent episodes go unreported, we believe our estimates on the presence and growth of violence in the area err on the conservative side.

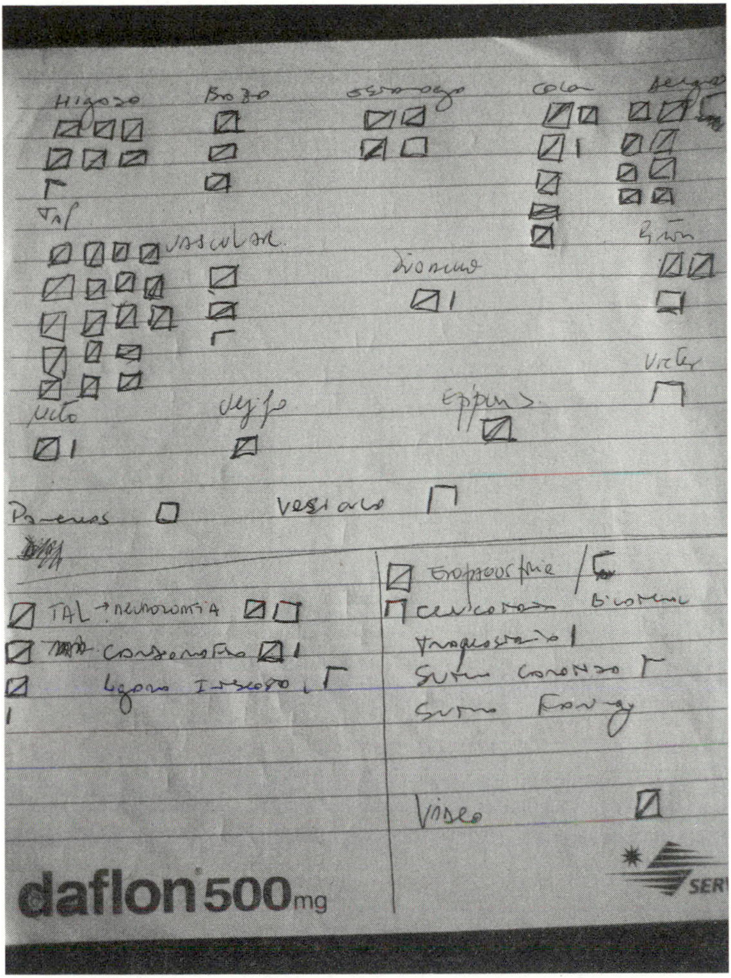

FIGURE 30. Keeping record: surgeries.

A last note on collaboration: Javier first visited the neighborhood twenty-five years ago when he was a young activist and worked in an after-school program in the area. Back in the late 1980s, the area was far from being as dangerous—for outsiders and insiders—as it is now. Between 2009 and 2012, he returned oftentimes to the neighborhood to conduct interviews and visit Fernanda at the local school, but he did not conduct the kind of ethnographic work that he had in the past for other research projects (Auyero 2000) or that Agustín carried out for this project. Although this admittedly eclectic combination of ethnographic work and team qualitative research was dictated more by necessity (professional and family obligations prevented Javier from spending a long time in the field) than by an explicit design, it has, for this particular case, distinctive advantages. Teamwork allows for the collection of data from different sources at similar points in time. This proved to be crucial in the reconstruction of the sequence of violent episodes. For example, Fernanda first heard about an event from her students, but given her own time constraints was unable to follow the story. Agustín would then pick up where Fernanda left off and relied on in-depth interviews with residents to reconstruct the longer string of events. *Cuatro ojos, ven más que dos*—as the Spanish saying goes—and two, and sometimes three, researchers hear more than one. Fernanda's unique embeddedness in the school and the level of trust between her and her students allowed her to collect valuable stories, but her role as a full-time teacher usually prevented her from following those accounts into the neighborhood. Outside the school, Agustín was able to do precisely this—track the progression of violence and examine its antecedents. Teamwork also enables the independent verification of data from different sources, as when we reconstructed the circumstances of a street fight or a homicide in their immediate aftermath by using the testimonies of youngsters and adults gathered by different researchers.

Teamwork then was neither carefully planned nor randomly improvised. Paraphrasing Karl Marx, we could say that we conducted research but, given the dangerous circumstances and the abundant practical constraints, not under conditions of our own choosing. We made, one could say, team virtue out of individual necessities. Had we waited until all the conditions for ideal ethnographic work were present for all three of us at the same time, this book would probably still be in the making.

LONG INTERVIEW GUIDE

How long have you lived in the neighborhood? Where did you live before? How did you decide to move here?

Compared to your previous neighborhood, how is this one? What do you like the most about this barrio? What do you dislike the most about this barrio?

Since you moved in, how has the neighborhood changed? Is it better or worse than before?

[If the interviewee speaks about violence, shootings, and/ or drugs]: How do you manage to avoid all this? What do you do with your sons/daughters? Do they stay inside? What do you do with them when they are not in school? Have you ever been mugged? Has your house ever been broken into? Tell us what happened.

What do your children like to do on the weekends? Do they leave the neighborhood? Where do they go?

Do you have relatives in the neighborhood? Do you receive help from them? Do they help you in raising your children?

Who takes care of your children when you go to work?

Do you receive any aid from the welfare office? Do you attend the local soup kitchen? If so, how often? Do you know who organizes the soup kitchen?

Is there someone in the household who is in prison? How long? Where is she/he?

Do you visit him/her? How often? How would you describe your relationship with him or her? Is it better or worse than before (when she/he was free)?

Do your sons/daughters go to visit him or her? Do they have friends who also have relatives behind bars?

Do you enjoy the visits? What do you like the most? What do you dislike the most?

How has life in the household changed since she/he went to prison? How did your life change?

FOCUS GROUP GUIDE (HIGH SCHOOL STUDENTS)

What do you like the most about the neighborhood? What do you dislike?

Where do you hang out on the weekends? Do you go to the city of Buenos Aires? Do you go by yourselves or in groups?

Have you ever been stopped by the police or gendarmes? When? Where? Describe in detail. Why do you think the police acted in that way?

We have heard from many adults that they are worried about drugs and violence. How do you manage at night? Are there "no go areas" in the neighborhood?

Have you ever been mugged? Describe in detail.

Do you work in La Salada? Describe what you do.

SHORT INTERVIEW QUESTIONNAIRE

We are doing a study for a professor at the University of Buenos Aires about living conditions in the neighborhood, and we want to ask you some questions. The information is confidential. We will not record your name.

NEIGHBORHOOD

1. Since you have lived here, how do you think the neighborhood has improved?
2. And how has it gotten worse?
3. What are the main problems in the neighborhood? (Please mention from high to low, and try to name three.)
4. Who would you say is the person or organization that most helps in the neighborhood? Who is the person or institution that most works to solve the problems you mentioned?

WORK

Now I am going to ask you some questions about your work.

5. In the last three months, the persons of this home have lived

1. by what they earn at work?	YES	NO
2. by any retirement or pension?	YES	NO
3. by severance pay?	YES	NO
4. by any government social subsidy?	YES	NO
5. by some social support from the church or other organization?	YES	NO
6. with merchandise, clothing, food from the government, church, school, etc.?	YES	NO

6. What do you do for work?
7. In what does your spouse or partner work?

8. Your work is

    a. a state employment program?
    b. a trial period?
    c. a fellowship/internship/learning opportunity?
    d. a stable job?
    e. none of the above (specify).

9. In that job do you have

    a. paid vacation?
    b. a holiday bonus?
    c. paid days of sick leave?
    d. health care?
    e. retirement (*descuento jubilatorio*)?
    f. none of the above.

10. Counting all the jobs of the people who live in the house, how much money comes into the house each month?

SOCIAL PROGRAMS

Now we are going to talk about social assistance.

11. Do you receive any social assistance (Asignación Universal, Plan Vida, etc.)?

    a. YES [Which ones?

    _____]
    b. NO [go to question 16]

12. How did you join?
13. Did someone invite you to sign up?

    a. YES [name of/relation to the person

    _____]
    b. NO

14. Did you go to any Unidad Básica, soup kitchen, or church to sign up?

    a. UB
    b. soup kitchen
    c. church
    d. other (specify).

15. If there is a problem with the assistance, who can you go see?

16. Do you or your children go to a soup kitchen?

    a. YES [Name of the soup kitchen

    _____]
    b. NO

17. If you or your son or daughter is sick, where do you go?
18. If you need medication, is there anyone in the neighborhood to whom you can go for free medicine?
19. Who is the most important political leader in the neighborhood? [Name_____]
20. What activities does he or she do for the neighborhood?
21. Is there anyone in the house/home who is detained (imprisoned)?
22. Since how long ago?
23. Do you go to visit them?
24. How often?
25. Do you go to visit him or her with your children?
26. If you have a child in school: What do you think could be the future occupation of your child who is in school?
27. What level of education does one need for that job?
28. Do you believe that he or she will live a life that is better, the same, or worse than the life you live now?

NOTES

INTRODUCTION

This book is a significantly revised and expanded version of a much shorter book that we published in Spanish two years ago under the title *La Violencia en los Márgenes*. Intended for a general audience, that book foregrounded the ethnographic evidence over the scholarly analysis. This book includes a significant amount of new ethnographic material and, just as important, it expands on the very preliminary, causal analysis delineated in the Spanish version. Unless otherwise noted, all translations from Spanish are our own.

1. Names of people and places have been changed to protect their anonymity.

2. The Conurbano is the area, comprised of thirty-three districts, that surrounds the city of Buenos Aires.

3. "Creció 50% el Abuso Sexual de Menores," *La Nación* online, February 24, 2008, http://www.lanacion.com.ar /990034-crecio-50-el-abuso-sexual-de-menores. On the diverse forms of violence experienced by the Argentine poor, see Bonaldi and del Cueto (2009); on fear of crime and perceptions of "inseguridad," see Kessler (2009). It is important to note, however, that although in the last three decades there has been a significant rise in crime, the overall crime rates in Argentina remain comparatively low (see United Nations Office on Drugs and Crime [UNODC] 2011).

4. Much like in the United States where the "concentration of violence goes hand in hand with the concentration of poverty" (Sharkey 2013:687), the Supreme Court report shows that there is a spatial clustering of homicides in and around neighborhoods with high levels of poverty (Corte Suprema de Justicia de la Nación [CSJN] 2013).

5. The pervasive violence experienced by those living at the urban margins may take a "chronic form" within marginalized communities (Brennan et al. 2007; Schwab-Stone et al. 1995). Clark and his colleagues (2007) refer to chronic exposure to violence as a "mental health hazard," referencing its harmful developmental, emotional, and behavioral impacts on individuals (Friday 1995; Holton 1995; Osofsky 1999; Farrell et al. 2007; Popkin et al. 2010). Ethnographic research also suggests that chronic exposure to violence and marginalization may influence individuals' schemes of perception, evaluation, and action (Bourgois and Schonberg 2009; Contreras 2012; T. Black 2009).

6. In his classic study of the US ghetto, Ulf Hannerz uses the notion of repertoire to describe the individuals' beliefs, values, and modes of action: "items of culture which are somehow stored" (1969:191) in them. Here I'm using the notion in a more restricted sense to focus attention on the deployment of violence as a repertoire of action. Coined and popularized by Charles Tilly to understand and explain patterns of collective claim-making across time and space, the notion of repertoire focuses on the set of routines by which people get together to act on their shared interests. The notion of repertoire brings together different levels of analysis ranging from large-scale changes, such as the development of capitalism (with the subsequent proletarianization of work) and the process of state making (with the parallel growth of the state's bulk, complexity, and penetration of its coercive and extractive power) to patterns of citizen-state interaction (Tilly 1986, 1995, 2006). Tilly's model exhorts us to conceptually hold together macrostructures and microprocesses by looking closely at the ways in which big changes indirectly shape collective action by affecting the interests, opportunities, organizations, and identities of ordinary people. Repertoires are both cultural and political constructs. They are "learned cultural creations, but they do not descend from abstract philosophy or take shape as a result of political propaganda; they emerge from struggle" (Tilly 1995:26). People "learn to break windows in protest, attack pilloried prisoners, tear down dishonored houses, stage public marches,

petition, hold formal meetings, organize special-interest associations. At any particular point in history, however, they learn only a rather small number of alternative ways to act together" (ibid.). This learned set of contentious routines, furthermore, is deeply political in that it: (a) emerges from continuous struggles against the state, (b) has an intimate relationship with everyday life and routine politics, and (c) is constrained by patterns of state repression. Scaled down and adapted to the study of urban violence, the theatrical metaphor of repertoire leads us to not only identify regularities in violent exchanges but also to examine their economic and political determinations and their cultural dimensions.

7. Our study was approved by the University of Texas at Austin IRB (protocol #2011–05–0126). Research participants (students, parents, and school authorities) were fully aware of Fernanda's dual role as teacher and researcher.

8. We wish to thank Daniel Brinks for making us aware of this risk in his insightful criticism of *La Violencia en los Márgenes*.

CHAPTER 1: EL BARRIO AND LA FERIA

1. Elena Peralta, "En el Riachuelo Hay Mucho Más Plomo que los Niveles Permitidos," *Clarín*, December 5, 2003.

2. In 2008, the Supreme Court ordered the cleanup of the Riachuelo. The court's ruling established that the federal government, the province of Buenos Aires, and the city of Buenos Aires were responsible for the prevention and restoration of the collective environmental damage existing in the Matanza-Riachuelo basin. The ruling mandated a series of obligatory actions to accomplish this goal, and created a broad system of control for the enforcement of the sentence, including the imposition of fines to state authorities.

3. For insightful accounts of the history and workings of these markets, see Hacher (2011) and Girón (2011).

4. "Un Emblema Mundial de lo Ilegal," *La Nación*, March 10, 2009, http://www.lanacion.com.ar/1107045-un -emblema-mundial-de-lo-ilegal.

5. See Cuvi, Jensen, and Auyero (2014) for a theoretical discussion of the role of violence in informal markets.

6. While the state facilitated the suburbanization of the poor by actively intervening in the housing market and in public transportation, it adopted a laissez-faire attitude with respect to the regulation of the urban land—the result of which is, according to Torres (1990), a very "fragmented and discontinuous" urban landscape.

7. Given the lack of reliable official data, considerable polemics revolve around existing figures. See reports by the Observatorio de la Deuda Social Argentina (http://www.uca.edu.ar/index.php/site/index/es/uca/observatorio-de-la-deuda-social-argentina).

8. On informal work as an alternative to un- and under-employment, see Fernández-Kelly and Shefner (2006).

9. Charles Bronson was a Hollywood actor frequently cast in the role of police officer or vigilante.

10. We use the term "civilizing process" in a restrictive way to refer to the process of the reduction of violence from the horizon of daily life. For elaborations and critiques of the larger notion of "civilizing process," see Aya (1978), Burkitt (1996), De Swaan (2001), Mennel (1990), and Pinker (2012). For its application to the case of the African American ghetto, see Wacquant (2004).

11. Violent specialists are actors who "often initiate violent political interaction, sometimes cause non-violent political interaction to turn violent, and frequently determine the outcome of political interaction, whether violent or otherwise" (Tilly 2003:5).

12. They also engage in various acts of solidarity: maintaining soup kitchens and a medical clinic, making clothing donations to the local hospital, and paying for private security for a local public school (Pogliaghi 2008:57).

13. "Linchan a un delincuente en Budge," *Crónica*, April 13, 2011.

14. "Ultimaron a Dos Hombres a Cuchilladas," *ArgenDiario*, April 15, 2011; and "Asesinan de una Puñalada a un Ciudadano Boliviano en Ingeniero Budge," *La Prensa*, April 26, 2011.

15. "Un Policía Federal Fue Asesinado por Delincuentes en Ingeniero Budge," *La Verdad*, October 18, 2011.

16. "Muerte en Budge," *Crónica*, January 21, 2012.

17. "Tiroteo Cerca de La Salada Provoca un Muerto," *Diario Popular*, May 28, 2012.

18. "Asesinaron de un Tiro en la Espalda a un Puestero de La Salada," *La Nación*, July 5, 2012, and "Aclaran que Asesinaron a un Feriante de La Salada Durante un Robo," *Télam*, July 6, 2012; and "Robó un Colectivo, se Tiroteó con la Policía y Murió," *InfoRegión*, July 3, 2012.

19. See "Asesinan de Balazo a un Joven de 18 Años; Hay un Sospechoso Herido," *La Nueva Provincia*, October 1, 2012; "Budge: Lo Matan Delante de Su Madre por Resistirse a un Robo," *Diario Popular*, October 2, 2012; "El Dueño de un Taller de Costura Fue Asesinado en Ingeniero Budge," *La Prensa*, October 6, 2012; and "Tiroteo en Budge," *Crónica*, October 1, 2012.

20. For journalistic reports on the effects of this drug among the marginalized youth, see Alexei Barrionuevo, "Lost in an Abyss of Drugs, and Entangled by Poverty," *New York Times*, July 29, 2009; Gustavo Barco, "Perderse en la Garras de la Muerte," *La Nación*, September 20, 2008; Kelly Hearn, "A New Scourge Sweeps through Argentine Ghettos: 'Paco.'" *Christian Science Monitor*, April 5, 2006. For an ethnographic account, see Epele (2010).

CHAPTER 2: BORN AMID BULLETS

1. For two paradigmatic examples from Latin America, see, for example, Rocha (2005) on "the traido" in Nicaragua and Linger (1990) on the Brazilian "briga." Although we did not detect it during our fieldwork, other ethnographic work describes how the logic of retaliation can lead to the logic of preemptive strike, further spinning violence. Sociologist David Smilde provides one example in the barrios of Caracas, Venezuela. Two years before Smilde interviewed thirty-two-year-old José Luis, the latter had been "shot by neighborhood thugs" while riding a friend's motorcycle: "One bullet entered his thigh, another his buttock. He managed to stay on the

motorcycle and get back home and then to a hospital. Though he recovered from his wounds, he was not out of danger: having been shot by someone meant that others, including the perpetrator, expected José Luis to seek revenge. And this meant that José Luis was a prime target for a pre-emptive strike" (2007:162).

2. Sebastián Hacher, "Crimen Mafioso: Un Penitenciario Fue Ejecutado a Sangre Fría en La Salada," *Tiempo Argentino*, August 4, 2010.

3. See Javier Auyero, "Deseos Urgentes," *Página/12*, March 19, 2012, www.pagina12.com.ar.

4. The following three stories are the product of Agustín's fieldwork.

5. Thieves, so the folk narrative goes, do not make deals with the police and are united in their collective hatred of cops. *Transas*, on the contrary, make all sorts of illicit arrangements with the police (*arreglan con la gorra*). Although the "thief vs. dealer" symbolic opposition organizes the moral universe of street crime (Alarcón 2003, 2009), in real life the boundaries between these two are less clear-cut. As our fieldwork taught us, people can be one or another at different points in time, and families may have members involved in both types of shady street entrepreneurship (see also Venkatesh 2009).

6. This is quite common in the province of Buenos Aires where 68 percent of inmates in state jails do not have a firm judicial sentence (i.e., they are imprisoned under pretrial detention) (Centro de Estudios Legales y Sociales [CELS] 2010).

CHAPTER 3: THE STATE AT THE MARGINS

1. Journalist Florencia Alcaraz conducted most of the interviews with police agents in this section. See Alcaraz and Auyero (2013) for a full account in Spanish.

2. In August 2009, Argentina's Supreme Court decriminalized the small-scale use of marijuana.

3. *Cabeza* or *cabecita negra* (literally, little black head) is a word used to disparage poor people who have black hair and

medium-dark skin, both migrants from northern Argentina and from other countries (Bolivia, for example).

4. On territorial stigma, see Wacquant (2007, 2008).

5. The term "liberated" means that the police forces purposefully cease to protect a specific geographic area, thus allowing criminal activity to flourish. For a full account of the effect of "liberated areas" in the course and effect of collective violence, see Auyero (2007).

6. For parallel accounts in Rio de Janeiro's favelas, see Gay (2005) and Perlman (2010). For ethnographic accounts of intermittent police presence in low-income communities in the United States, see Bourgois (1995), Venkatesh (2000), and, more recently, Rios (2010).

7. On the relationship between the Bonaerense police and car theft, see Dewey (2010, 2012); see also Sain (2008).

8. On "political defection" and "police appropriation" of the issue of public security, see Sain (2008).

9. The film *El Bonaerense* provides a very insightful and, according to the literature, accurate rendition of the way in which illegality is institutionalized in the police force. Learning to be a cop, the film shows, implies by necessity learning to be a delinquent—above and beyond the good intentions of new recruits.

10. For a recent illuminating journalistic report, see Alarcón (2013). See also the documentary *No Me Cabe Tu Gorra* (available at http://www.youtube.com/watch?v=hxtAIsg317M).

11. On the expansion of drug consumption and trafficking (particularly cocaine) in Argentina and other countries of the Southern Cone (Uruguay and Brazil) during the past decade, see Pontón (2013). As Sain (2013) describes: "In the last decade, the steady growth of illegal drug consumption, in particular of cocaine, in the large cities of Argentina favored the gradual formation of a growing retail market, diversified and highly profitable, whose supply was provided through a diversified structure of drug dealing. This expansion is explained through a series of cultural and economic conditions and dispositions but also by a crucial factor: the proliferation of 'kitchens' in which cocaine began being produced

locally. The acquisition in neighboring countries of cocaine paste and its movement across the border, the easy access to the necessary chemical precursors and the learning of the elaboration of cocaine hydrochloride, offered local drug groups the opportunity to become producers."

12.   The state's intermittent and frantic presence in Buenos Aires' urban margins is akin to the one described by Dennis Rodgers for the case of Managua, a state presence that incarnates a "qualitatively different form of state governmentality, based on the ability to repeatedly precipitate localized 'states of exception' through terrorizing raids that symbolically demonstrate the arbitrary power of the state" (2006:325).

13.   Police action is virtually absent when it comes to intervening in widespread, illegal child labor; many of Fernanda's students (all of them younger than thirteen) work in the nearby street fair either transporting, selling, and/or manufacturing goods in unmonitored sweatshops.

14.   We want to thank Randol Contreras for making us aware of this point.

CHAPTER 4: ETHICS AND POLITICS AMID VIOLENCE

1.   Highlighting the role that religion plays in addressing violence in the barrios of Caracas, David Smilde writes: "By becoming Evangelical, the individual is effectively extracted from extended violent interaction" (2007:5). Though the Catholic Church and Evangelicalism have a strong presence in Arquitecto Tucci, and as attentive as our observations and interviews were to the ethical dimension, we did not detect any signs that religion provided men or women "with a way to step-out of conflict-ridden situations" (ibid. 6).

2.   While Elliot and Aseltine rely on interviews to learn about mother's protective carework practices, our ethnographic methods point to the way these practices embed themselves in the daily lives of people living amid precarity and widespread violence.

3. See also Nikki Jones's (2009) work on the African American ghetto and her description of how mothers teach daughters to become able fighters, under the belief that they are transmitting valuable skills for survival in marginalized, destitute neighborhoods.

4. Nikki Jones describes a slightly similar phenomenon. Young girls in the African American ghetto, "may use the criminal justice system to negotiate violence in their relationships; however, for many girls, activating the criminal justice system is not an end in itself. Rather, it is a tool to be used in a multistage process of protecting oneself from an immediate threat of abuse" (2009:149).

5. "Tres Jóvenes Matan a Piedrazos a un Hombre en Ingeniero Budge," *Diario Popular*, February 4, 2013.

CONCLUSION: TOWARD A POLITICAL SOCIOLOGY OF URBAN MARGINALITY

1. The image of the oil spill can be problematic and misleading in that it may imply that violence stands outside an otherwise fully peaceful, functional society. Violence, in world-historical terms, is an aspect of social life, not something that exists separate from, and occasionally disrupts, the social order. Violence, the pages of this book show, is both constitutive and destructive. We want to thank David Smilde and Dennis Rodgers for pointing out this tension in our analysis. The image of the oil spill is meant to evoke not a general conception of violence but a more limited understanding of the ways in which violence becomes pervasive in social interactions at a certain time and place.

2. For similar arguments, see Wacquant (2008) and Goffman (2009).

3. The state makes itself present in the area in ways other than the police, such as a plethora of meager social assistance programs (the largest one being, as noted, the cash transfer program known as Asignación Universal por Hijo), many public schools, and the local hospital. Important as they are for the survival of the local population, we did not detect any

influence of these forms of state presence in the dynamics of interpersonal violence.

4.   From the work of Megan Comfort (2008), for example, we learn that the prison regulates poor people's daily lives in visible and not so visible ways. The prison "socializes" not only those who are behind bars but also their partners, relatives, and loved ones who regularly come in contact with it and end up "doing time together." From the work of Goffman (2009), we are now discovering the horrifying effects that incarceration is having in the everyday lives of those living in poor African American communities. The generalized fear, the mutual suspicion, and the feeling of being constantly "on the run" pervade the lives of marginalized youngsters as they sometimes evade and other times resist the state's "punishment of the poor" (Wacquant 2008).

5.   On the epistemic preference for easily codable data, see Kalyvas (2003).

6.   See "Colombia's Houses of Justice," available at www.restorativejustice.org/editions/2003/July/housesofjustice.

7.   The phrase "21st Century Welfare" is the apt expression that economist Lena Lavinas uses to refer to the "wider continental tendency to concentrate social spending on cash transfers rather than expanding provision of decommodified services" (2013:32). In what Jamie Peck and Nik Theodore (2010) recently called a veritable transnational "fast-policy" development, these conditional cash transfer programs (CCTs) have become the main strategy to deal with urban and rural poverty. According to Lavinas's critique of CCTs, they all "operate on a residual basis, as a safety net to compensate for market failures," and "no Latin American country has transformed them into rights guaranteeing a minimum income. They provide some compensation to the needy, yet they remain disconnected from anti-cyclical and permanent redistributive policies—a constitutive element of any system of universal social protection" (2013:24).

BIBLIOGRAPHY

Adams, Vincanne. 2013. *Markets of Sorrow, Labors of Faith: New Orleans in the Wake of Katrina.* Durham, NC: Duke University Press.

Alarcón, Cristian. 2003. *Cuando Me Muera Quiero que Me Toquen Cumbia: Vidas de Pibes Chorros.* Buenos Aires: Norma.

Alarcón, Cristian. 2009. *Si Me Querés Quereme Transa.* Buenos Aires: Norma.

Alarcón, Cristian. 2013. "La Violencia de la Bonaerense," http://www.lacampora.org/2013/12/13/la-violencia-de-la -bonaerense.

Alcaraz, Florencia, and Javier Auyero. 2013. "Violencia en Budge: Policías en Acción." *Revista Anfibia.* October.

Al-Mohammad, Hayder, and Daniela Peluso. 2012. "Ethics and the 'Rough Ground' of the Everyday: The Overlappings of Life in Postinvasion Iraq." *Journal of Ethnographic Theory* 2 (2): 42–58.

Altimir, Oscar, Luis Beccaria, and Martín Gonzales Rozada. 2002. "Income Distribution in Argentina, 1974–2002." *Cepal Review* 78 (December): 1–32.

Amnistía Internacional. 2008. *Muy Tarde, Muy Poco: Mujeres Desprotegidas ante la Violencia de Género en Argentina.* Buenos Aires: Amnistía Internacional Argentina.

Anderson, Elijah. 1999. *Code of the Street: Decency, Violence, and the Moral Life of the Inner City*. New York: W. W. Norton.

Arditti, Rita. 1999. *Searching for Life: The Grandmothers of the Plaza de Mayo and the Disappeared Children of Argentina*. Berkeley: University of California Press.

Arendt, Hannah. 1970. *On Violence*. New York: Harcourt Brace Jovanovich.

Arias, Desmond. 2006. *Drugs and Democracy in Rio de Janeiro: Trafficking, Social Networks, and Public Security*. Chapel Hill, NC: University of North Carolina Press.

Arias, Desmond, and Daniel Goldstein (editors). 2010. *Violent Democracies in Latin America*. Durham, NC: Duke University Press.

Aricapa, Ricardo. 2005. *Comuna 13: Crónica de una Guerra Urbana*. Colombia: Universidad de Antioquía.

Armstrong, Gary. 1998. *Football Hooligans: Knowing the Score*. Oxford: Berg.

Arondskin, Ricardo. 2001. *¿Más Cerca o Más Lejos del Desarrollo? Transformaciones Económicas en los 90*. Buenos Aires: Centro Rojas.

Auyero, Javier. 2000. *Poor People's Politics*. Durham, NC: Duke University Press.

Auyero, Javier. 2007. *Routine Politics and Collective Violence in Argentina: The Gray Zone of State Power*. New York: Cambridge University Press.

Auyero, Javier. 2010. "Visible Fists, Clandestine Kicks, and Invisible Elbows: Three Forms of Regulating Neoliberal Poverty." *European Review of Latin American and Caribbean Studies* 8:5–26.

Auyero, Javier. 2012. *Patients of the State*. Durham, NC: Duke University Press.

Auyero, Javier, and Débora Swistun. 2009. *Flammable: Environmental Suffering in an Argentine Shantytown*. New York: Oxford University Press.

Auyero, Javier, and María Fernanda Berti. 2013. *La Violencia en los Márgenes*. Buenos Aires: Katz Ediciones.

Aya, Rod. 1978. "Norbert Elias and 'The Civilizing Process.'" *Theory and Society* 5 (2): 219–28.

Ayala, Alex, and Jorge Derpic. 2013. "Bolivia: Los Linchados de el Alto." *Revista Anfibia*, http://www.revistaanfibia.com/cronica/bolivia-los-linchados-de-el-alto.

Baird, Adam. 2012. "The Violent Gang and the Construction of Masculinity amongst Socially Excluded Young Men." *Safer Communities* 11 (4).

Bandura, Albert. 1982. "Self-Efficacy Mechanism in Human Agency." *American Psychologist* 37 (2): 122–47.

Bandura, Albert. 1998. "Personal and Collective Efficacy in Human Adaptation and Change." In *Advances in Psychological Science*, ed. J. G. Adair, D. Belanger, and K. L. Dion. Vol. 1, *Personal, Social, and Cultural Aspects*, 51–71. Hove, UK: Psychology Press.

Bayat, Asef. 1997. *Street Politics*. New York: Columbia University Press.

Becker, Howard. 1958. "Problems of Inference and Proof in Participant Observation." *American Sociological Review* 23:652–60.

Becker, Howard. 1970. *Sociological Work: Methods and Substance*. Chicago: Aldine.

Bernstein, Richard. 2013. *Violence: Thinking without Banisters.* New York: Wiley.

Black, Donald. 1983. "Crime as Social Control." *American Sociological Review* 48:34–45.

Black, Timothy. 2009. *When a Heart Turns Rock Solid: The Lives of Three Puerto Rican Brothers On and Off the Streets.* New York: Vintage.

Blok, Anton. 2001. *Honor and Violence.* Oxford: Blackwell.

Bloom, S. 2003. "The Sanctuary Model: A Trauma-Informed Systems Approach to the Residential Treatment of Children." *Residential Group Care Quarterly* 4 (2): 1–4.

Bloom, S. 1997. *Creating Sanctuary: Toward the Evolution of Sane Societies.* New York: Routledge.

Bonaldi, Pablo, and Carla del Cueto. 2009. "Fragmentación y Violencia en Dos Barrios de Moreno." In *La Vida Política en los Barrios Populares de Buenos Aires*, ed. Alejandro Grimson, Cecilia Ferraudi Curto, and Ramiro Segura, 103–28. Buenos Aires: Prometeo Libros.

Bourdieu, Pierre. 1998. *Practical Reason: On the Theory of Action.* Stanford, CA: Stanford University Press.

Bourdieu, Pierre. 2000. *Pascalian Meditations.* Stanford, CA: Stanford University Press.

Bourgois, Philippe. 1995. *In Search of Respect: Selling Crack in El Barrio.* New York: Cambridge University Press.

Bourgois, Philippe. 2009. "Recognizing Invisible Violence: A Thirty-Year Ethnographic Retrospective." In *Global Health in Times of Violence*, edited by Barbara Rylko-Bauer, Linda Whiteford, and Paul Farmer, 18–49. Santa Fe, NM: School of Advanced Research Press.

Bourgois, Philippe, and Jeff Schonberg. 2009. *Righteous Dopefiend*. Berkeley: University of California Press.

Bouvard, Marguerite Guzman. 1994. *Revolutionizing Motherhood: The Mothers of the Plaza de Mayo*. Wilmington, DE: Scholarly Resources.

Bratingham, Patricia, and Paul Bratingham. 1993. "Nodes, Paths, and Edges: Considerations on the Complexity of Crime and the Physical Environment." *Journal of Environmental Psychology* 13:3–28.

Braun, Bruce, and James McCarthy. 2005. "Hurricane Katrina and Abandoned Being." *Environment and Planning D: Society and Space* 23 (6): 802–9.

Brennan, Robert, Beth Molnar, and Feltron Earls. 2007. "Refining the Measurement of Exposure to Violence (ETV) in Urban Youth." *Journal of Community Psychology* 35 (3): 603–18.

Briceño-León, Roberto. 1999. "Violence and the Right to Kill: Public Perceptions from Latin America." Unpublished manuscript, available at http://lanic.utexas.edu/project/etext/violence/memoria/session_1.html.

Brinks, Daniel. 2008. *The Judicial Response to Police Violence in Latin America: Inequality and the Rule of Law*. New York: Cambridge University Press.

Britton, Dana. 2011. *The Gender of Crime*. New York: Rowman & Littlefield.

Brown, Phil. 1991. "The Popular Epidemiology Approach to Toxic Waste Contamination." In *Communities at Risk: Collective Responses to Technological Hazards*, edited by Stephen Robert Couch and J. Stephen Kroll-Smith, 133–55. New York: Peter Lang.

Brown, Phil, Steve Kroll-Smith, and Valerie J. Gunter. 2000. "Knowledge, Citizens, and Organizations: An Overview of Environments, Diseases, and Social Conflict." In *Illness and the Environment: A Reader in Contested Medicine*, edited by Steve Kroll-Smith, Phil Brown, and Valerie J. Gunter, 9–25. New York: New York University Press.

Brush, Lisa. 2011. *Poverty, Battered Women, and Work in U.S. Public Policy*. New York: Oxford University Press.

Bryson, Lois, Kathleen McPhillips, and Kathryn Robinson. 2001. "Turning Public Issues into Private Troubles: Lead Contamination, Domestic Labor, and the Exploitation of Women's Unpaid Labor in Australia." *Gender and Society* 15 (5): 754–72.

Burawoy, Michael et al. 1991. *Ethnography Unbound: Power and Resistance in the Modern Metropolis*. Berkeley: University of California Press.

Burkitt, Ian. 1996. "Civilization and Ambivalence." *British Journal of Sociology* 47 (1): 135–50.

Caldeira, Teresa. 2000. *City of Walls: Crime, Segregation, and Citizenship in Sao Paulo*. Berkeley: University of California Press.

Calvo, Ernesto, and María Victoria Murillo. 2004. "Who Delivers? Partisan Clients in the Argentine Electoral Market. *American Journal of Political Science* 48 (4): 742–57.

Castells, Manuel. 1984. *The City and the Grassroots*. Berkeley: University of California Press.

Castillo Berthier, Hector, and Gareth Jones. 2009. "Mean Streets: Gangs, Violence and Daily Life in Mexico City." In *Youth Violence in Latin America: Gangs and Juvenile*

Justice in Perspective, edited by Gareth A. Jones and Dennis Rodgers. New York: Palgrave-Macmillan.

Centro de Estudios Legales y Sociales (CELS). 2009. *Derechos Humanos en Argentina: Informe 2009*. Buenos Aires: Siglo XXI.

Centro de Estudios Legales y Sociales (CELS). 2010. "Denuncia Incumplimiento, Propone Medidas, Solicita Audiencia Pública," http://www.cels.org.ar/common /documentos.

Centro de Estudios Legales y Sociales (CELS). 2012. *Derechos Humanos en Argentina*. Informe 2012. Buenos Aires: Siglo XXI.

Clark, Cheryl, Louise Ryan, Ichiro Kawachi, Marina Canner, Lisa Berkman, and Rosalind Wright. 2007. "Witnessing Community Violence in Residential Neighborhoods: A Mental Health Hazard for Urban Women." *Journal of Urban Health: Bulletin of the New York Academy of Medicine* 85 (1): 22–38.

Collins, Randall. 2008. *Violence: A Micro-Sociological Theory*. Princeton, NJ: Princeton University Press.

Comfort, Megan. 2008. *Doing Time Together*. Chicago: University of Chicago Press.

Contreras, Randol. 2012. *The Stickup Kids: Race, Drugs, Violence and the American Dream*. Berkeley: University of California Press.

Cooney, Paul. 2007. "Argentina's Quarter-Century Experiment with Neoliberalism: From Dictatorship to Depression." *Revista de Economia Contemporanea* 11 (1): 7–37.

Coordinadora Contra la Represión Policial e Institucional (CORREPI). 2012. *Archivo de Casos.* Buenos Aires: CORREPI.

Corte Suprema de Justicia de la Nación (CSJN). 2013. "Informe Homicidios Dolosos 2012," http://www.csjn.gov .ar/investigaciones.

Cravino, María Cristina, Juan Pablo del Rio, and Juan Ignacio Duarte. 2008. "Magnitud y Crecimiento de las Villas y Asentamientos en el Área Metropolitana de Buenos Aires en los Últimos 25 Años." Paper presented at the XIV Encuentro de la Red Universitaria Latinoamericana de Cátedras de Vivienda—Facultad de Arquitectura, Urbanismo y Diseño—Universidad de Buenos Aires, October 1–4, 2008.

Cuvi, Jacinto, Katherine Jensen, and Javier Auyero. 2014. "Violence and Pacification in Informal Markets." Unpublished manuscript, Ethnography Lab, Sociology Department, University of Texas at Austin.

D'Angiolillo, Julián, Marcelo Dimentstein, Martín Di Peco, Ana Isabel Guérin, Adriana Laura Massidda, Constanza Molíns, Natalia Muñoa, Juan Pablo Scarfi, and Pío Torroja. 2010. "Feria La Salada: Una Centralidad Periférica Intermitente en el Gran Buenos." In *Argentina: Persistencia y Diversificación, Contrastes e Imaginarios en las Centralidades Urbanas*, edited by M. Gutman, 182–96. Quito: Olacchi.

Damaske, Sarah. 2010. *For the Family? How Class and Gender Shape Women's Work.* New York: Oxford University Press.

Darnton, Robert. 2006. *The Great Cat Massacre and Other Episodes in French Cultural History.* New York: Basic Books.

Daroqui, Alcira (editor). 2009. *Muertes Silenciadas.* Buenos Aires: Centro Cultural de la Cooperación.

Das, Veena, ed. 1990. *Mirrors of Violence: Communities, Riots, and Survivors in South Asia*. Oxford: Oxford University Press.

Das, Veena. 2012. "Ordinary Ethics: The Perils and Pleasures of Everyday Life." In *A Companion to Moral Anthropology*, edited by D. Fassin, 133–49. New York: Wiley-Blackwell.

Davis, Natalie. 1973. "The Rites of Violence: Religious Riot in Sixteenth-Century France." *Past and Present* 59 (May): 51–91.

Davis, Mike. 2006. *Planet of Slums*. London: Verso.

DeBoard-Lucas, Renee, and John Grych. 2011. "Children's Perceptions of Intimate Partner Violence: Causes, Consequences, and Coping." *Journal of Family Violence* 26 (5): 343–54.

De Swaan, Abram. 2001. "Dyscivilization, Mass Extermination, and the State." *Theory, Culture & Society* 18 (2–3): 265–76.

Desmond, Matthew. 2010. *On the Fireline: Living and Dying with Wildland Firefighters*. Chicago: Chicago University Press.

Dewey, Matias. 2010. "Fragile States, Robust Structures: Illegal Police Protection in Buenos Aires." Working paper. Leibniz: GIGA Research Programme Unit, Institute of Latin American Studies.

Dewey, Matias. 2012. "Illegal Police Protection and the Market for Stolen Vehicles in Buenos Aires." *Journal of Latin American Studies* 44 (4): 679–702.

Dewey, Matias. 2014. "Taxing the Shadows: A Political Economy of Sweatshops in La Salada, Argentina."

Unpublished manuscript, Max Planck Institute for the Study of Societies.

Dirección Nacional de Política Criminal (DNPC). 2008. "Hechos Delictuosos Registrados: 2008." Buenos Aires: Ministerio de Justicia, Seguridad y Derechos Humanos.

Drakulich, Kevin M., and Robert D. Crutchfield. 2013. "The Role of Perceptions of the Police in Informal Social Control: Implications for the Racial Stratification of Crime and Control." *Social Problems* 60 (3): 383–407.

Eden, Lynn. 2004. *Whole World on Fire: Organizations, Knowledge and Nuclear Weapons Devastation.* Ithaca, NY: Cornell University Press.

Edin, Kathryn, and Maria Kefalas. 2005. *Promises I Can Keep: Why Poor Women Put Motherhood Before Marriage.* Berkeley: University of California Press.

Ehrensaft, M. K., P. Cohen, J. Brown, E. Smailes, H. Chen, and J. G. Johnson. 2003. "Intergenerational Transmission of Partner Violence: A 20-Year Prospective Study." *Journal of Consulting and Clinical Psychology* 71:741–53.

Elias, Norbert. 1978. "On Transformations of Aggressiveness." *Theory and Society* 5 (2): 229–42.

Elias, Norbert. 1994. *The Civilizing Process.* Oxford, UK: Blackwell.

Elliot, Sinikka, and Elyshia Aseltine. 2013. "Raising Teenagers in Hostile Environments: How Race, Class and Gender Matter for Mothers' Protective Carework." *Journal of Family Issues* 34 (6): 719–44.

Emerson, Robert, Rachel Fretz, and Linda Shaw. 1995. *Writing Ethnographic Fieldnotes.* Chicago: University of Chicago Press.

Epele, María. 2010. *Sujetar por la Herida: Una Etnografía Sobre Drogas, Pobreza y Salud*. Buenos Aires: Paidós.

Fanon, Franz. 1990. *The Wretched of the Earth*. New York: Penguin Classics.

Farmer, Paul. 2004. "An Anthropology of Structural Violence." *Current Anthropology* 45 (3): 305–17.

Farrell, Albert D., Elizabeth H. Erwin, Kevin W. Allison, Aleta Meyer, Terri Sullivan, Suzanne Camou, Wendy Kliewer, and Layla Esposito. 2007. "Problematic Situations in the Lives of Urban African American Middle School Students: A Qualitative Study." *Journal of Research on Adolescence* 17 (2): 413–54.

Fernández-Kelly, Patricia, and Jon Shefner. 2006. *Out of the Shadows: Political Action and the Informal Economy in Latin America*. University Park: Pennsylvania State University Press.

Fishman, Robert. 1989. *Bourgeois Utopias: The Rise and Fall of Suburbia*. New York: Basic Books.

Ford, Richard. 2012. *Canada*. Scarborough, Ontario: HarperCollins.

Fosco, G. M., R. L. DeBoard, and J. H. Grych. 2007. "Making Sense of Family Violence: Implications of Children's Appraisals of Interparental Aggression for Their Short- and Long-term Functioning." *European Psychologist* 12:6–16.

Friday, Jennifer. 1995. "The Psychological Impact of Violence in Underserved Communities." *Journal of Health Care for the Poor and Underserved* 6 (4): 403–9.

Garbarino, James. 1993. "Children's Response to Community Violence: What Do We Know?" *Infant Mental Health Journal* 14 (2): 103–15.

Gay, Robert. 2005. *Lucia: Testimonies of a Brazilian Drug Dealer's Woman*. Philadelphia: Temple University Press.

Geertz, Clifford. 1973. *The Interpretation of Cultures*. New York: Basic Books.

Gelles, Richard. 1985. "Family Violence." *Annual Review of Sociology* 11:347–67.

Geurts, Kathryn. 2003. *Culture and the Senses: Bodily Ways of Knowing in an African Community*. Berkeley: University of California Press.

Giraudy, Agustina. 2007. "The Distributive Politics of Emergency Employment Programs in Argentina." *Latin American Research Review* 42 (2): 33–55.

Girón, Nacho. 2011. *La Salada: Radiografía de la Feria más Polémica de Latinoamérica*. Buenos Aires: Ediciones B.

Glymph, Thavolia. 2008. *Out of the House of Bondage: The Transformation of the Plantation Household*. New York: Cambridge University Press.

Goffman, Alice. 2009. "On the Run: Wanted Men in a Philadelphia Ghetto." *American Sociological Review* 74 (3): 339–57.

Goffman, Alice. 2014. *On the Run: Fugitive Life in an American City*. Chicago: University of Chicago Press.

Goffman, Erving. 1969. *Where the Action Is*. New York: Allen Lane.

Goldstein, Daniel. 2012. *Outlawed: Between Security and Rights in a Bolivian City*. Durham, NC: Duke University Press.

Goldstein, Donna. 1998. "Nothing Bad Intended: Child Discipline, Punishment, and Survival in a Shantytown in Rio de Janeiro, Brazil." In *Small Wars: The Cultural Politics of Childhood*, edited by N. Scheper-Hughes and C. Sargent, 389–415. Berkeley: University of California Press.

Goldstein, Donna. 2003. *Laughter Out of Place*. Berkeley: University of California Press.

Goldstein, Paul J. 1985. "The Drugs/Violence Nexus: A Tripartite Conceptual Framework." *Journal of Drug Issues* 14:493–506.

Goldstein, Paul J., Henry H. Brownstein, Patrick J. Ryan, and Patricia Bellucci. 1997. "Crack and Homicide in New York City: A Case Study in Epidemiology of Violence." In *Crack in America: Demon Drugs and Social Justice*, edited by Craig Reinarman and Harry G. Levine, 113–30. Berkeley: University of California Press.

Gould, Roger. 2003. *Collision of Wills: How Ambiguity about Social Rank Breeds Conflict*. Chicago: University of Chicago Press.

Gowan, Teresa. 2010. *Hobos, Hustlers, and Backsliders: Homeless in San Francisco*. Minneapolis: University of Minnesota Press.

Guerra, Nancy, Rowell Huesmann, and Anja Spindler. 2003. "Community Violence Exposure, Social Cognition and Aggression among Urban Elementary School Children." *Child Development* 74 (5):1561–76.

Gupta, Akhil. 1995. "Blurred Boundaries: The Discourse of Corruption, the Culture of Politics, and the Imagined State." *American Ethnologist* 22 (2): 375–402.

Gupta, Akhil. 2005. "Narratives of Corruption: Anthropological and Fictional Accounts of the Indian State." *Ethnography* 6 (1): 5–34.

Hacher, Sebastián. 2011. *Sangre Salada*. Buenos Aires: Marea Editorial.

Hannerz, Ulf. 1969. *Soulside: Inquiries into Ghetto Culture and Community*. Lund: Berlingska Boktryckeriet.

Haney, Lynne. 1996. "Homeboys, Babies, and Men in Suits: The State and the Reproduction of Male Dominance." *American Sociological Review* 61 (5): 759–78.

Harding, David. 2010. *Living the Drama: Community, Conflict, and Culture among Inner-City Boys*. Chicago: University of Chicago Press.

Harvey, David. 2005. *A Brief History of Neoliberalism*. New York: Oxford University Press.

Hautzinger, Sarah. 2007. *Violence in the City of Women: Police and Batterers in Bahia, Brazil*. Berkeley: University of California Press.

Hays, Sharon. 1996. *The Cultural Contradictions of Motherhood*. New Haven, CT: Yale University Press.

Heimer, Carol. 1988. "Social Structure, Psychology, and the Estimation of Risk." *Annual Review of Sociology* 14:491–519.

Heimer, Carol. 2001. "Cases and Biographies: An Essay on Routinization and the Nature of Comparison." *Annual Review of Sociology* 27:47–76.

Helmke, Gretchen, and Stephen Levitsky. 2004. "Informal Institutions and Comparative Politics." *Perspectives in Politics* 2:725–40.

Hochschild, Arlie, and Anne Manchung. 1990. *The Second Shift*. New York: Penguin Books.

Holton, John. 1995. "Witnessing Violence: Making the Invisible Visible." *Journal of Health Care for the Poor and Underserved* 6 (2): 152–59.

Holston, James. 2008. *Insurgent Citizenship*. Princeton, NJ: Princeton University Press.

Hume, Mo. 2009. *The Politics of Violence: Gender, Conflict, and Community in El Salvador*. Malden, MA: Wiley-Blackwell.

Imbusch, Peter, Michel Misse, and Fernando Carrión. 2011. "Violence Research in Latin America and the Caribbean: A Literature Review." *International Journal of Conflict and Violence* 5 (1): 87–154.

Isla, Alejandro, and Daniel Miguez (editors). 2003. *En Los Márgenes de la Ley*. Buenos Aires: Paidós.

Jackman, Mary. 2002. "Violence in Social Life." *Annual Review of Sociology* 28:387–415.

Jacobs, Bruce, and Richard Wright. 2006. *Street Justice: Retaliation in the Criminal World*. New York: Cambridge University Press.

Jacobs, Bruce. 2004. "A Typology of Street Criminal Retaliation." *Journal of Research in Crime and Delinquency* 41 (3): 295–323.

Jerolmack, Colin, and Shamus Khan. 2014. "Talk Is Cheap: Ethnography and the Attitudinal Fallacy." *Sociological Methods and Research* 43 (2): 178–209.

Jones, Gareth, and Dennis Rodgers (editors). 2009. *Youth Violence in Latin America: Gangs and Juvenile Justice in Perspective*. New York: Palgrave.

Jones, Nikki. 2009. *Between Good and Ghetto: African American Girls and Inner-City Violence*. New Jersey: Rutgers University Press.

Kakar, Sudhir. 1996. *The Colors of Violence: Cultural Identities, Religion, and Conflict*. Chicago: University of Chicago Press.

Kalyvas, Stathis. 2003. "The Ontology of 'Political Violence': Action and Identity in Civil Wars." *Perspectives on Politics* 1:475–94.

Katz, Jack. 1982. "A Theory of Qualitative Methodology: The Social System of Analytic Fieldwork." In *Poor People's Lawyers in Transition*, edited by J. Katz, 197–218. New Brunswick, NJ: Rutgers University Press.

Katz, Jack. 1988. *Seductions of Crime*. New York: Basic Books.

Katz, Jack. 2001. "From How to Why: On Luminous Description and Causal Inference in Ethnography (Part I)." *Ethnography* 2 (4): 443–73.

Katz, Jack. 2002. "From How to Why: On Luminous Description and Causal Inference in Ethnography (Part II)." *Ethnography* 3 (1): 73–90.

Kelly, Liz. 1988. *Surviving Sexual Violence*. Cambridge, UK: Polity.

Keohane, Robert. 1986. "Reciprocity in International Relations." *International Organization* 40 (1): 1–27.

Kessler, Gabriel. 2009. *El Sentimiento de Inseguridad*. Buenos Aires: Siglo XXI.

Kirk, David, and Andrew Papachristos. 2011. "Cultural Mechanisms and the Persistence of Neighborhood Violence." *American Journal of Sociology* 116 (4): 1190–1233.

Klinenberg, Eric. 2008. *Heat Wave*. Chicago: Chicago University Press.

Koonings, Kees. 2001. "Armed Actors, Violence and Democracy in Latin America in the 1990s." *Bulletin of Latin American Research* 20 (4): 401–8.

Koonings, Kees, and Dirk Kruijt (editors). 2007. *Fractured Cities: Social Exclusion, Urban Violence and Contested Spaces in Latin America*. London: Zed Books.

Korbin, Jill. 2003. "Children, Childhoods, and Violence." *Annual Review of Anthropology* 32:431–46.

Kornhauser, Ruth R. 1984. *Social Sources of Delinquency: An Appraisal of Analytic Models*. Chicago: University of Chicago Press.

Kotlowitz, Alex. 1991. *There Are No Children Here: The Story of Two Boys Growing Up in the Other America*. New York: Anchor Books.

Krug, Etienne G., Linda L. Dahlberg, James A. Mercy, Anthony B. Zwi, and Rafael Lozano (editors). 2002. *World Report on Violence and Health*. Geneva: World Health Organization.

Kurst-Swanger, Karel, and Jacqueline Petcosky (editors). 2003. *Violence in the Home: Multidisciplinary Perspectives*. New York: Oxford University Press.

Lambek, Michael, ed. 2010. *Ordinary Ethics: Anthropology, Language, and Action*. New York: Fordham University Press.

Lamont, Michelle, and Virag Molnár. 2002. "The Study of Boundaries across the Social Sciences." *Annual Review of Sociology* 28:167–95.

Lavinas, Lena. 2013. "21st Century Welfare." *New Left Review* 84:5–40.

Lazar, Sian. 2008. *El Alto, Rebel City: Self and Citizenship in Andean Bolivia*. Durham, NC: Duke University Press.

Lazaric, Nathalie. 2000. "The Role of Routines, Rules, and Habits in Collective Learning: Some Epistemological and Ontological Considerations." *European Journal of Economic and Social Systems* 14 (2): 157–71.

LeBlanc, Adrian. 2004. *Random Family: Love, Drugs, Trouble, and Coming of Age in the Bronx*. New York: Scribner.

Levenson, Deborah. 2013. *Adiós Niño: The Gangs of Guatemala City and the Politics of Death*. Durham, NC: Duke University Press.

Levey, Cara, Daniel Ozarow, and Chistopher Wylde (editors). 2014. *Argentina since the 2001 Crisis: Recovering the Past, Reclaiming the Future*. London: Palgrave.

Levi, Primo. 1986. *The Drowned and the Saved*. New York: Vintage.

Linger, Daniel. 1990. "Essential Outlines of Crime and Madness: Man-Fights in São Luís." *Cultural Anthropology* 5 (1): 62–77.

Logan, John. 2003. "Life and Death in the City: Neighborhoods in Context." *Contexts* 2 (2): 30–40.

Logan, John, and Harvey Molotch. 1987. *Urban Fortunes: The Political Economy of Place*. Berkeley: University of California Press.

Lunecke Reyes, Alejandra. 2008. *La Paradoja de Santa Adriana: Tráfico de Drogas en una Población Emblemática*. Tesis de Magister en Desarrollo Urbano, Instituto de Estudios

Urbanos y Territoriales, Pontificia Universidad Católica de Chile, Facultad de Arquitectura, Diseño y Estudios Urbanos.

Macmillan, Ross. 2001. "Violence and the Life Course: The Consequences of Victimization for Personal and Social Development." *Annual Review of Sociology* 27:1–22.

Margolin, Gayla, and Elana Gordis. 2000. "The Effects of Family and Community Violence on Children." *Annual Review of Psychology* 51:445–79.

Massey, Douglas, and Nancy Denton. 1993. *American Apartheid: Segregation and the Making of the Underclass.* Cambridge, MA: Harvard University Press.

Mauss, Marcel. 1979 [1916]. *Seasonal Variations of the Eskimo: A Study in Social Morphology* (in collaboration with Henri Beuchat). Boston: Routledge and Kegan Paul.

Mauss, Marcel. 2000. *The Gift.* New York: Norton.

McCart, Michael, Daniel Smith, Benjamin Saunders, Dean Kilpatrick, Heidi Resnick, and Kenneth Ruggiero. 2007. "Do Urban Adolescents Become Desensitized to Community Violence? Data from National Survey." *American Journal of Orthopsychiatry* 77 (3): 434–42.

McCann, Bryan. 2014. *Hard Times in the Marvelous City: From Dictatorship to Democracy in the Favelas of Rio de Janeiro.* Durham, NC: Duke University Press.

Menjívar, Cecilia. 2011. *Enduring Violence: Ladina Women's Lives in Guatemala.* Berkeley: University of California Press.

Mennell, Stephen. 1990. "Decivilising Processes: Theoretical Significance and Some Lines of Research." *International Sociology* 5 (2): 205–33.

Moser, Caroline, and Cathy McIlwaine. 2004. *Encounters with Violence in Latin America.* New York: Taylor and Francis.

Muggah, Robert. 2012. *Researching the Urban Dilemma: Urbanization, Poverty and Violence.* Canada: IDRC.

Müller, Markus-Michael. 2011. "The Rise of the Penal State in Latin America." *Contemporary Justice Review* 15 (1): 57–76.

Müller, Markus-Michael. 2012. "Addressing an Ambivalent Relationship: Policing and the Urban Poor in Mexico City." *Journal of Latin American Studies* 44 (2): 319–46.

Mullins, Christopher, Richard Wright, and Bruce Jacobs. 2004. "Gender, Street Life and Criminal Retaliation." *Criminology* 42 (4): 911–40.

Murray, Joseph, David Farrington, Ivana Sekol, and Rikke Olsen. 2009. "Effects of Parental Imprisonment on Child Antisocial Behaviour and Mental Health: A Systematic Review." *Campbell Systematic Reviews* 4:1–105.

National Public Radio. 2010. "'Making Toast': Simple Gestures for Moving On." NPR Books, http://www.npr.org/templates/story/story.php?storyId=123610749.

Neumann, Pamela J. 2013. "The Gendered Burden of Development in Nicaragua." *Gender & Society* 27 (6): 799–820.

Newman, Katherine, and Rebekah Peeples Massengill. 2006. "The Texture of Hardship: Qualitative Sociology of Poverty, 1995–2005." *Annual Review of Sociology* 32:423–46.

Nichter, Simeon. 2008. "Vote Buying or Turnout Buying? Machine Politics and the Secret Ballot." *American Political Science Review* 102 (1): 19–31.

Noveck, Jocelyn. 2012. "Amid Chaos, Manhattanites Seek Comfort in Routines." Associated Press online, http://bigstory.ap.org/article/amid-chaos-manhattanites-seek-comfort-routines.

Observatorio de la Deuda Social Argentina (ODSA). 2011. "El Problema de la Inseguridad en la Argentina: Factores que Influyen en la Delincuencia y Disparan el Sentimiento de Inseguridad o Miedo a Ser Víctima de un Delito." Buenos Aires: Pontificia Universidad Católica Argentina.

O'Donnell, Guilermo. 1993. "On the State, Democratization and Some Conceptual Problems: A Latin American View with Glances at Some Postcommunist Countries." *World Development* 21:1355–69.

O'Neill, Kevin, and Kedron Thomas (editors). 2011. *Securing the City: Neoliberalism, Space, and Insecurity in Postwar Guatemala.* Durham, NC: Duke University Press.

Osofsky, Joy. 1999. "The Impact of Violence on Children." *Domestic Violence and Children* 9 (3): 33–49.

Ousey, Graham, and Matthew Lee. 2002. "Examining the Conditional Nature of the Illicit Drug Market–Homicide Relationship: A Partial Test of the Theory of Contingent Causation." *Criminology* 40 (1): 73–102.

Papachristos, Andrew. 2009. "Murder by Structure: Dominance Relations and the Social Structure of Gang Homicide." *American Journal of Sociology* 115 (1): 74–128.

Parker, Robert N., and Kathleen Auerhahn. 1998. "Alcohol, Drugs, and Violence." *Annual Review of Sociology* 24:291–311.

Pearce, Jenny. 2010. "Perverse State Formation and Securitized Democracy in Latin America." *Democratization* 17 (2): 286–386.

Peck, Jamie, and Nik Theodore. 2010. "Recombinant Workfare across the Americas." *Geoforum* 41 (2): 195–208.

Pellow, David. 2002. *Garbage Wars: The Struggle for Environmental Justice in Chicago*. Cambridge, MA: MIT Press.

Penglase, Ben. 2010. "The Owner of the Hill: Masculinity and Drug-trafficking in Rio de Janeiro, Brazil." *Journal of Latin American and Caribbean Anthropology* 15 (2): 317–37.

Perlman, Janice. 2010. *Favela: Four Decades of Living on the Edge in Rio de Janeiro*. New York: Oxford University Press.

Pinker, Steven. 2012. *The Better Angels of Our Nature: Why Violence Has Declined*. New York: Penguin.

Pírez, Pedro. 2001. "Buenos Aires: Fragmentation and Privatization of the Metropolitan City." *Environment and Urbanization* 14 (1): 145–58.

Pogliaghi, Leticia. 2008. "Informalidad Urbana: Una Aproximación a Partir de un Estudio de Caso; Las Ferias de La Salada, Lomas de Zamora (2006–2007)." Master's thesis, School of Politics and Government, Universidad Nacional de San Martín, Buenos Aires.

Ponce de León-Calero, Alejandro. 2014. *Que la Muerte se Haga Esperar: Cotidianeidad y Confrontación Armada en una Barriada de Medellín*. Retrieved from https://www.academia.edu/2450788/Que_la_muerte_se_haga_ esperar _Cotidianidad_y_confrontacion_armada_en_una_barriada _de_Medellin_2009_-_2012.

Pontón, Daniel. 2013. "La Economía del Narcotráfico y Su Dinámica en América Latina." *Íconos* 47:135–53.

Popkin, Susan, Tama Leventhal, and Gretchen Weismann. 2010. "Girls in the 'Hood: How Safety Affects the Life

Chances of Low-Income Girls." *Urban Affairs Review* 45 (6): 715–44.

Portes, Alejandro. 1972. "Rationality in the Slum: An Essay in Interpretive Sociology." *Comparative Studies in Society and History* 14 (3): 268–86.

Portes, Alejandro, and Bryan R. Roberts. 2005. "The Free-Market City: Latin American Urbanization in the Years of the Neoliberal Experiment." *Studies in Comparative International Development* 40 (1): 43–82.

Prieur, Annick. 1998. *Mema's House: Mexico City; On Transvestites, Queens, and Machos.* Chicago: University of Chicago Press.

Programa de las Naciones Unidas para el Desarrollo (PNUD). 2013. *Seguridad Ciudadana con Rostro Humano: Diagnostico y Propuestas para América Latina.* New York: PNUD.

Puex, Nathalie. 2003. "Las Formas de la Violencia en Tiempos de Crisis: Una Villa Miseria del Conurbano Bonaerense." In *Heridas Urbanas: Violencia Delictiva y Transformaciones Sociales en los Noventa.* Buenos Aires: Editorial de las Ciencias.

Reding, Nick. 2009. *Methland: The Death and Life of an American Small Town.* New York: Bloomsbury.

Reinarman, Craig, and Harry G. Levine (editors). 1997. *Crack in America: Demon Drugs and Social Justice.* Berkeley: University of California Press.

Reiss, Albert, and Jeffrey A. Roth. 1993. *Understanding and Preventing Violence.* Washington, DC: National Academic Press.

Rios, Victor. 2010. *Punished: Policing the Lives of Black and Latino Boys.* New York: New York University Press.

Robinson, William. 2008. *Latin America and Global Capitalism: A Critical Globalization Perspective.* Baltimore: Johns Hopkins University Press.

Rocha, José Luis. 2005. "El Traido: Clave de la Continuidad de las Pandillas." *Envío* 280:35–41.

Rock, David. 1987. *Argentina, 1516–1982: From Spanish Colonization to Alfonsin.* Berkeley: University of California Press.

Rodgers, Dennis. 2006. "Living in the Shadow of Death: Gangs, Violence and Social Order in Urban Nicaragua, 1996–2002." *Journal of Latin American Studies* 38:267–92.

Rodgers, Dennis. 2009. "Slum Wars of the 21st Century: Gangs, Mano Dura, and the New Urban Geography of Conflict in Central America." *Development and Change* 40 (5): 949–76.

Rodgers, Dennis, and Bruce O'Neill. 2012. "Infrastructural Violence: Introduction to the Special Issue." *Ethnography* 13 (4): 401–12.

Rodgers, Dennis, Jo Beall, and Ravi Kanbur (editors). 2012. *Latin American Urban Development into the 21st Century: Towards a Renewed Perspective on the City.* New York: Palgrave.

Rodríguez, Cesar, and Rodrigo Uprimny. 2014. "¿Justicia para Todos o Seguridad para el Mercado? El Neoliberalismo y la Reforma Judicial en Colombia y América Latina." Unpublished manuscript, available at www.juecesyfiscales.org.

Rosenblatt, Roger. 2010. *Making Toast.* New York: HarperCollins.

Rotker, Susana. 2002. *Citizens of Fear: Urban Violence in Latin America.* New Brunswick, NJ: Rutgers University Press.

Rutter, Michael. 1987. "Psychological Resilience and Protective Mechanisms." *American Journal of Orthopsychiatry* 57 (3): 316–31.

Sain, Marcelo. 2004. *Política, Policía y Delito: La Red Bonaerense.* Buenos Aires: Capital Intelectual.

Sain, Marcelo. 2008. *El Leviatán Azul.* Buenos Aires: Siglo XXI.

Sain, Marcelo. 2009. "El Fracaso del Control de la Drogas Ilegales en Argentina." *Nueva Sociedad* 222:132–46.

Sain, Marcelo. 2013. "Las Grietas del Doble Pacto." *Le Monde Diplomatique*, http://www.eldiplo.org/174-el-desafio-narco/las-grietas-del-doble-pacto.

Salvia, Agustín. 2007. "Consideraciones Sobre la Transición a la Modernidad, la Exclusión Social y la Marginalidad Económica: Un Campo Abierto a la Investigación Social y al Debate Político." In *Sombras de una Marginalidad Fragmentada: Aproximaciones a la Metamorfosis de los Sectores Populares de la Argentina*, edited by Agustín Salvia and Eduardo Chávez Molina, 25–66. Buenos Aires: Miño y Dávila.

Salvia, Agustín. 2013. "Heterogeneidades Estructurales y Desigualdades Sociales Persistentes: De la Caída del Modelo Neoliberal a la Falta de Horizontes Bajo el Modelo Neodesarrollista." Available at http://www.uca.edu.ar/index.php/site/index/es/uca/observatorio-de-la-deuda-social-argentina.

Sampson, Robert. 1985. "Neighborhood and Crime: The Structural Determinants of Personal Victimization." *Journal of Research in Crime and Delinquency* 22:7–40.

Sampson, Robert. 1987. "Urban Black Violence: The Effect of Male Joblessness and Family Disruption." *American Journal of Sociology* 93:348–82.

Sampson, Robert. 2012. *Great American City: Chicago and the Enduring Neighborhood Effect.* Chicago: Chicago University Press.

Sampson, Robert, and Byron Groves. 1989. "Community Structure and Crime: Testing Social-Disorganization Theory." *American Journal of Sociology* 94 (4): 774–802.

Sampson, Robert, Stephen W. Raudenbush, and Felton Earls. 1997. "Neighborhoods and Violent Crime: A Multilevel Study of Collective Efficacy." *Science* 277:918–24.

Scarfi, Juan Pablo, and Martín Di Peco. 2011. "Assessing the Current Challenges of La Salada Fair in Greater Buenos Aires: Towards a New Agenda for Urban and Political Design." Unpublished manuscript, Cambridge University.

Scheper-Hughes, Nancy. 1992. *Death Without Weeping: The Violence of Everyday Life in Brazil.* Berkeley: University of California Press.

Scheper-Hughes, Nancy. 1996. "Peace-Time Crimes." *Social Identities* 3 (3): 471–97.

Scheper-Hughes, Nancy. 1997. "Small Wars and Invisible Genocides." *Social Science and Medicine* 43 (5): 889–900.

Scheper-Hughes, Nancy, and Philippe Bourgois (editors). 2003. *Violence in War and Peace.* Malden, MA: Blackwell.

Schneider, Jane, and Peter Schneider. 2003. *Reversible Destiny: Mafia, Antimafia, and the Struggle for Palermo.* Berkeley: California University Press.

Schwab-Stone, Mary E., Tim S. Ayers, Wesley Kasprow, Charlene Voyce, Charles Barone, Timothy Shriver, and Robert P. Weissberg. 1995. "No Safe Haven: A Study of Violence Exposure in an Urban Community." *Journal of the American Academy of Child and Adolescent Psychiatry* 34:1343–52.

Scott, James. 1985. *Weapons of the Weak: Everyday Forms of Peasant Resistance.* New Haven, CT: Yale University Press.

Secor, Anna. 2007. "Between Longing and Despair: State, Space and Subjectivity in Turkey." *Environment and Planning D: Society and Space* 25:33–52.

Segura, Ramiro. 2009. "'Si vas a venir a una villa, loco, entrá de otra forma': Distancias Sociales, Límites Espaciales, y Efectos de Lugar en un Barrio Segregado del Gran Buenos Aires." In *La Vida Política en los Barrios Populares de Buenos Aires*, ed. Alejandro Grimson, Cecilia Ferraudi Curto, and Ramiro Segura, 41–62. Buenos Aires: Prometeo Libros.

Sharkey, Patrick, Nicole Tirado-Strayer, Andrew Papachristos, and Cybele Raver. 2012. "The Effect of Local Violence on Children's Attention and Impulse Control." *American Journal of Public Health* 120 (12): 2287–93.

Sharkey, Patrick. 2010. "The Acute Effect of Local Homicides on Children's Cognitive Performance." *Proceedings of the National Academy of Sciences* 107:11733–38.

Sharkey, Patrick. 2013. *Stuck in Place: Urban Neighborhoods and the End of Progress toward Racial Equality.* Chicago: University of Chicago Press.

Shaw, Clifford, and Henry McKay. 1942. *Juvenile Delinquency and Urban Areas*. Chicago: University of Chicago Press.

Shay, Jonathan. 1994. *Achilles in America*. New York: Atheneum.

Shklar, Judith N. 1985. *Ordinary Vices*. Cambridge, MA: Harvard University Press.

Smilde, David. 2007. *Reasons to Believe: Cultural Agency in Latin American Evangelicalism*. Berkeley: University of California Press.

Snodgrass Godoy, Angelina. 2002. "Lynchings and the Democratization of Terror in Postwar Guatemala: Implications for Human Rights." *Human Rights Quarterly* 24 (3): 640–61.

Steinberg, Marc. 1999. *Fighting Words: Working-Class Formation, Collective Action, and Discourse in Early Nineteenth-Century England*. Ithaca, NY: Cornell University Press.

Stokes, Susan. 2005. "Perverse Accountability: A Formal Model of Machine Politics with Evidence from Argentina." *American Political Science Review* 99 (3): 315–25.

Svampa, Maristella. 2001. *Los que Ganaron: La Vida en los Countries y en los Barrios Privados*. Buenos Aires: Biblios.

Szwarcberg, Mariela. 2010. "Clientelismo en Democracia: Lecciones del Caso Argentino." *Nueva Sociedad* 225:139–55.

Teubal, Miguel. 2004. "Rise and Collapse of Neoliberalism in Argentina: The Role of Economic Groups." *Journal of Developing Societies* 20 (3–4): 173–88.

Thistle, Susan. 2006. *From Marriage to the Marketplace: The Transformation of Women's Lives and Work*. Berkeley: University of California Press.

Thompson, E. P. 1994. *Customs in Common*. New York: New Press.

Tilly, Charles. 1986. *The Contentious French*. Cambridge, MA: Harvard University Press.

Tilly, Charles. 1992. *Coercion, Capital, and European States*. New York: Wiley-Blackwell.

Tilly, Charles. 1995. "Contentious Repertoires in Great Britain." In *Repertoires and Cycles of Collective Action*, edited by Mark Traugott. Durham, NC: Duke University Press.

Tilly, Charles. 2003. *The Politics of Collective Violence*. New York: Cambridge University Press.

Tilly, Charles. 2006. *Regimes and Repertoires*. Chicago: University of Chicago Press.

Tilly, Charles. 2008. *Credit and Blame*. Princeton, NJ: Princeton University Press.

Tolan, Patrick, Deborah Gorman-Smith, and David Henry. 2006. "Family Violence." *Annual Review of Psychology* 57:557–83.

Torres, Horacio A. 1990. "El Mapa Social de Buenos Aires (1940–1990)." Facultad de Arquitectura, Diseño y Urbanismo, Dirección de Investigaciones.

Torresi, Leonardo. 1998. "Ingeniero Budge, Una de las Zonas Más Temibles del País." *Clarín*, November 29.

Turpin, Jennifer, and Lester Kurtz. 1997. *The Web of Violence*. Chicago: University of Illinois Press.

United Nations Office on Drugs and Crime (UNODC). 2011. *Global Study on Homicide: Trends, Contexts, Data*. Vienna: UNODC.

Venkatesh, Sudhir. 2000. *American Project: The Rise and Fall of a Modern Ghetto.* Cambridge, MA: Harvard University Press.

Venkatesh, Sudhir. 2008. *Gang Leader for a Day: A Rogue Sociologist Takes to the Streets.* New York: Penguin.

Venkatesh, Sudhir. 2009. *Off the Books: The Underground Economy of the Urban Poor.* Cambridge, MA: Harvard University Press.

Verbitsky, Horacio. 2011. "¿Seguriqué?" *Página12 Digital.* March 6.

Villalón, Roberta. 2007. "Neoliberalism, Corruption, and Legacies of Contention: Argentina's Social Movements, 1993–2006." *Latin American Perspectives* 34 (2): 139–56.

Villarreal, Ana. Forthcoming. "The Logistics of Fear: Drug Violence and Everyday Life in Monterrey, Mexico." In *Violence at the Urban Margins*, edited by Javier Auyero, Philippe Bourgois, and Nancy Scheper-Hughes. New York: Oxford University Press.

Villarreal, Andrés. 2002. "Political Competition and Violence in Mexico: Hierarchical Social Control in Local Patronage Structures." *American Sociological Review* 67 (4): 477–98.

Voisin, Dexter, J. D. Bird, M. Hardestry, and Cheng Shi Shiu. 2011. "African American Adolescents Living and Coping with Community Violence on Chicago's Southside." *Journal of Interpersonal Violence* 26 (12): 2483–98.

Volkov, Vadim. 2002. *Violent Entrepreneurs: The Use of Force in the Making of Russian Capitalism.* Ithaca: Cornell University Press.

Wacquant, Loïc. 2002. "Scrutinizing the Street: Poverty, Morality, and the Pitfalls of Urban Ethnography." *American Journal of Sociology* 107 (6): 1468–1532.

Wacquant, Loïc. 2003. "Ethnografeast: A Progress Report on the Practice and Promise of Ethnography." *Ethnography* 4:5–14.

Wacquant, Loïc. 2004. "Decivilizing and Demonizing: The Social and Symbolic Remaking of the Black Ghetto and Elias in the Dark Ghetto." In *The Sociology of Norbert Elias*, edited by Steven Loyal and Stephen Quilley, 95–121. New York: Cambridge University Press.

Wacquant, Loïc. 2005. "Carnal Connections: On Embodiment, Apprenticeship, and Membership." *Qualitative Sociology* 28 (4): 445–74.

Wacquant, Loïc. 2007. *Urban Outcasts: A Comparative Sociology of Advanced Marginality*. London: Polity.

Wacquant, Loïc. 2008. "The Militarization of Urban Marginality: Lessons from the Brazilian Metropolis." *International Political Sociology* 2:56–74.

Walton, Marsha, Alexis Harris, and Alice Davidson. 2009. "'It Makes Me a Man from the Beating I Took': Gender and Aggression in Children's Narratives about Conflict." *Sex Roles* 61:383–98.

Ward, Peter M., Edith R. Jiménez Huerta, Erika Grajeda, and Claudia Ubaldo Velázquez. 2011. "'The House that Mum and Dad Built': Self-Help Housing Policies for Second Generation Inheritance and Succession." *Habitat International* 35:467–85.

Weitz-Shapiro, R. 2006. "Partisanship and Protest: The Politics of Workfare Distribution in Argentina." *Latin American Research Review* 41:122–47.

Wilding, Polly. 2010. "'New Violence': Silencing Women's Experiences in the Favelas of Brazil." *Journal of Latin American Studies* 42:719–47.

Wilding, Polly. 2013. *Negotiating Boundaries: Gender, Violence, and Transformation in Brazil.* Hampshire, UK: Palgrave/ Macmillan.

World Health Organization (WHO). 2002. *World Report on Violence and Health.* Geneva: World Health Organization.

Zonabend, Francoise. 1993. *The Nuclear Peninsula.* New York: Cambridge University Press.

Zubillaga, Verónica. 2009. "'Gaining Respect': The Logic of Violence among Young Men in the Barrios of Caracas, Venezuela." In *Youth Violence in Latin America: Gangs and Juvenile Justice in Perspective,* ed. Gareth Jones and Dennis Rodgers. New York: Palgrave.

Zubillaga, Verónica, Manuel Llorens, and John Souto. Forthcoming. "*Chismosas* and *Alcahuetas*: Being the Mother of an Empistolado within the Everyday Armed Violence of a Caracas *Barrio.*" In *Violence at the Urban Margins,* edited by Javier Auyero, Philippe Bourgois, and Nancy Scheper-Hughes. New York: Oxford University Press.

INDEX